PRESENTED BY

David Williams
in honor of:
Elizabeth Hemphill

SMYTHE GAMBRELL LIBRARY

WESTMINSTER SCHOOLS

2002

David Boyd

NATIONS OF THE WORLD

ISRAEL

Jen Green

RAINTREE
STECK-VAUGHN
PUBLISHERS

A Harcourt Company

Austin   New York
www.steck-vaughn.com

Steck-Vaughn Company

First published 2001 by Raintree Steck-Vaughn Publishers,
an imprint of Steck-Vaughn Company.
Copyright © 2001 Brown Partworks Limited.

Library of Congress Cataloging-in-Publication Data

Green, Jen
    Israel / Jen Green.
        p. cm -- (Nations of the world)
    Includes bibliographical references (p.) and index.
    ISBN 0-7398-1286-6
    1. Israel -- Juvenile literature. [1. Israel.] I. Title. II. Nations of the world (Austin, Tex.)

    DS118.G876 2000
    956.94--dc21

                                                    00-031079

Printed and bound in the United States
1 2 3 4 5 6 7 8 9 0 BNG 05 04 03 02 01 00

Brown Partworks Limited
Editors: Robert Anderson, Peter Jones
Designer: Joan Curtis
Cartographers: Colin Woodman and William Le
    Bihan
Picture Researcher: Brenda Clynch
Editorial Assistant: Roland Ellis
Indexer: Kay Ollerenshaw

Raintree Steck-Vaughn
Publishing Director: Walter Kossmann
Art Director: Max Brinkmann

Front cover: Overview of Eilat (background); bedouin woman (below right); gilt menorah (top left)
Title page: Jaffa town harbor

The acknowledgments on p. 128 form part of this copyright page.

Contents

Foreword

Since ancient times, people have gathered together in communities where they could share and trade resources and strive to build a safe and happy environment. Gradually, as populations grew and societies became more complex, communities expanded to become nations—groups of people who felt sufficiently bound by a common heritage to work together for a shared future.

Land has usually played an important role in defining a nation. People have a natural affection for the landscape in which they grew up. They are proud of its natural beauties—the mountains, rivers, and forests—and of the towns and cities that flourish there. People are proud, too, of their nation's history—the shared struggles and achievements that have shaped the way they live today.

Religion, culture, race, and lifestyle, too, have sometimes played a role in fostering a nation's identity. Often, though, a nation includes people of different races, beliefs, and customs. Many may have come from distant countries. Nations have rarely been fixed, unchanging things, either territorially or racially. Throughout history, borders have changed, often under the pressure of war, and people have migrated across the globe in search of a new life or because they are fleeing from oppression or disaster. The world's nations are still changing today: Some nations are breaking up and new nations are forming.

The region now covered by the nation of Israel has one of the best-documented histories in the world. It is the site of the earliest town—Jericho—and a center for three of the world's religions—Judaism, Christianity, and Islam. However, the state of Israel was only formed in 1948 as a homeland for the Jewish people and the first years of its existence were a struggle to establish both farming and industry in the fledgling state. These early years were marked too by a series of wars with its Arab neighbors. More recently, years of economic growth and the ongoing peace process have boosted the region, bringing stability and the prospect of a lasting agreement with its neighbors and the Palestinians.

Introduction

ISRAEL

Israel is a small country in the far southwest of Asia, bordering the Mediterranean Sea. It lies in the Middle East—a term loosely used to describe the countries of southwest Asia and northeast Africa. The nations on Israel's borders—Lebanon, Syria, Jordan, and Egypt—are all Arab countries.

Israel came into being only in 1948 and was created as a homeland for the Jewish people. Since 1948, many Jews have emigrated to Israel from other countries, particularly from Eastern Europe, Russia, and the United States. The history of the country, however, goes back much further. The region that today makes up Israel is often called the Holy Land. In ancient times, it was known as Palestine or, in the Bible, as Canaan. It is sacred ground for Jews, Christians, and Muslims. Judaism, the Jewish religion, and Christianity both began there. According to the book of Genesis in the Bible, Abraham, the father of the Hebrews—the ancient Jewish people—lived in what is now Israel. Later, the region was conquered by many different peoples, including the Romans, who took it over in 63 B.C. In A.D. 135, after the Jews had twice rebelled against Roman rule, the Romans drove many Jews out of the Holy Land.

The Jewish people dispersed and set up communities in different countries around the world. This event is

Israel's short spring quickly produces a green landscape and abundant flowers, most of which perish in the scorching summer heat.

7

The 20-shekel banknote has a picture of Moshe Sharett, second prime minister of Israel.

called the Diaspora, which means "dispersion." In their new homes all over the world, and through the centuries, Jews have suffered persecution and racism. So many dreamed of returning to their people's ancient homeland.

Meanwhile, the land of Palestine passed into the hands of other conquerors. Muslim Arabs ruled the land from 640 to 1099, followed by Christian Crusaders. The Ottoman Turks ruled from 1517 to 1917. Beginning in the late 1800s, a Jewish movement called Zionism campaigned to establish a Jewish country in Palestine. Increasing numbers of Jews began to emigrate to Palestine. Their return caused conflict with the people already living there, the Palestinian Arabs. Arabs had lived in the region for over a thousand years.

The Israeli flag consists of a six-pointed star, the Star of David, on a white background with two blue stripes. The stripes represent the Jewish prayer shawl (a garment worn by Orthodox Jews).

Before, during, and after World War II (1939–1945), thousands of Jews fled persecution and systematic extermination in Nazi Europe (*see* p. 69) and returned to Palestine. In 1947, the United Nations (UN) proposed that Palestine be divided into separate Jewish and Arab nations. Arabs opposed the creation of a Jewish state. In 1948, the Jewish State of Israel was proclaimed, but was immediately attacked by its Arab neighbors.

Since this time, there have been repeated conflicts between Israel and its neighbors (*see* pp. 70–77). More recently, both sides have taken steps to resolve these differences. In 1979, Israel made peace with Egypt and returned the Sinai Peninsula. In 1993, it signed a peace agreement with the Palestinian Liberation Organization (PLO), which was fighting for a Palestinian Arab

POPULATION DENSITY

Israel's population is concentrated in the fertile coastal plain and around the country's main cities. To the south, the desert is virtually uninhabited, apart from a small nomadic population. Recently the government has offered incentives to those willing to settle in the desert areas

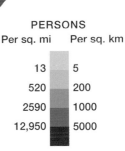

PERSONS	
Per sq. mi	Per sq. km
13	5
520	200
2590	1000
12,950	5000

homeland. This paved the way for Israel to withdraw from Arab areas in the West Bank and Gaza Strip. In 1994, Israel made peace with Jordan. However, there is still a long way to go before conflict in the Middle East region is resolved.

Israel's population has increased steadily due to mass immigration of Jews from around the world. In the 1990s there was an upsurge with the immigration of Russian Jews after the collapse of the Soviet Union.

Israel is a small nation that could fit into a corner of many American states. It has few natural resources. Since 1948, war and unrest have put pressures on the country's economy. Nonetheless, Israel has succeeded in modernizing its industry and agriculture and has transformed large areas of former desert into farmland. It has also improved education, health care, and transportation and is in the forefront of many areas of scientific and medical research. Israelis now enjoy a high standard of living and have one of the longest life expectancies in the world.

The People of Israel

Israel's population stands at just under six million. It is a fairly densely populated country, with an average of 699 people per square mile (269 people per sq. km). However, the population is not evenly spread

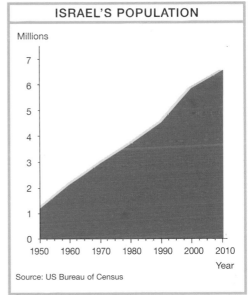

ISRAEL'S POPULATION

Millions

Source: US Bureau of Census

POPULATION BY AGE

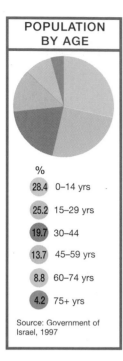

%	
28.4	0–14 yrs
25.2	15–29 yrs
19.7	30–44
13.7	45–59 yrs
8.8	60–74 yrs
4.2	75+ yrs

Source: Government of Israel, 1997

Israel's population is overwhelmingly young, a fact due to repeated waves of immigration. The vast majority of immigrants to Israel have been under fifty.

Above is the word "Israeli" written in the Hebrew script. The script is read from right to left .

throughout the country. An overwhelming 93 percent of Israelis live in towns and cities, leaving only 7 percent of the population in the countryside. Israel has a young population, with an average age of only 26.

In 1948, the population of Israel was 806,000, of which 650,000 were Jews. Since then, over two million Jews have emigrated (moved) to Israel from around the world. Israel's population is now 80.5 percent Jewish. Almost all of the remaining 19.5 percent are Arabs.

Israeli Jews can be divided into two main groups. Ashkenazi Jews are descended from Jewish communities in Central and Eastern Europe. Sephardi Jews come from the Mediterranean region, the Middle East, and North Africa. Jews born in Israel are nicknamed *sabrah* (plural, *sabrot*). The name refers to the prickly pear, a fruit that is prickly on the outside but sweet on the inside. Only half of all Jews in Israel are *sabrot*.

Israeli Arabs are mostly Palestinian Arabs. They include Muslims and Christians, and also Druze and bedouin. The Druze are an Arabic-speaking people who developed their own religion 800 years ago. They live in northern Israel. The bedouin are a nomadic (wandering) people who live in the desert in the south. They may cross borders into other countries, but are generally tied to one area of the desert by their knowledge of the local terrain and water supply.

Israel is a democratic republic. Its official name is the State of Israel. Here, the word "state" is used in its sense of "nation" rather than a part of a bigger country, as in the United States. Israel's parliament, the Knesset, governs the country from the capital,

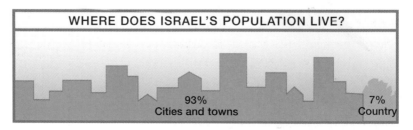

WHERE DOES ISRAEL'S POPULATION LIVE?

93% Cities and towns

7% Country

The National Anthem

The lyrics of the Israeli national anthem, "*HaTikah,*" meaning "The Hope," express the Jewish people's yearning for a homeland. Its words were composed in 1878 by Naftali Herz Imber (1856–1909). The music was written by Samuel Cohen and is based on folk tunes of Romania and Moldavia. The English translation is as follows:

As long as deep in the heart,
The soul of a Jew yearns,
And toward the East
An eye looks to Zion,
Our hope is not yet lost,
The hope of two thousand years,
To be a free people in our land,
The land of Zion and Jerusalem.

To be a free people in our land,
The land of Zion and Jerusalem.

Jerusalem. Israel has no written constitution, but has a series of basic laws that control how the government rules. All Israelis over the age of 18 can vote in elections.

During its short history, Israel has been at war many times. It spends heavily on its armed forces. The army, navy, and air force are all combined in a single organization, the Israeli Defense Force (IDF), which is one of the best-trained military forces in the world. When they reach the age of 18, all eligible Jewish men and women must serve in the IDF. Men serve for three years, women for 18 months.

Many Jews follow the Jewish religion of Judaism, of these the most devout are the Orthodox. Today, however, many ethnic Jews are also secular, or nonreligious.

Languages and Symbols
People speak many different languages in Israel, but Hebrew—the ancient Jewish language—and Arabic are the official languages. English, Russian, and Yiddish—a German dialect that has been spoken by European Jews for centuries—are also commonly heard. When Israel was set up, most people knew only a little Hebrew from religious instruction, or none at all. The language had to be revived for modern usage (*see* p. 96).

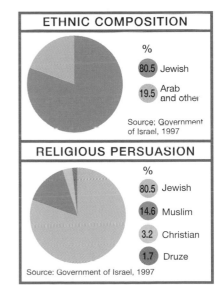

ETHNIC COMPOSITION

%
80.5 Jewish
19.5 Arab and other

Source: Government of Israel, 1997

RELIGIOUS PERSUASION

%
80.5 Jewish
14.6 Muslim
3.2 Christian
1.7 Druze

Source: Government of Israel, 1997

Land and Cities

"If the state does not put an end to the desert, the desert will put an end to the state."

Israel's first prime minister David Ben-Gurion

Israel lies on a narrow strip of land at the junction of Africa and Asia. The Mediterranean Sea forms Israel's western border. Lebanon and Syria lie to the north and northeast. The kingdom of Jordan lies to the east. The Sinai Peninsula, part of Egypt, lies to the southwest. To the south, a narrow wedge of Israeli land stretches down to the Gulf of Aqaba, the eastern arm of the Red Sea.

Israel is a tiny country, occupying just 8,017 square miles (20,770 sq. km). This makes it only slightly larger than New Jersey. In addition, since 1967 Israel has occupied a further 3,939 square miles (10,100 sq. km) of territory: the Golan Heights, the West Bank, and the Gaza Strip. The Golan Heights to the northeast belong to Syria. The West Bank in the east is so-named because it lies on the west bank of the Jordan River. The United Nations originally set the territory aside for Palestinian Arabs but the area was occupied by Israel in the 1967 war. Since then, many Israelis have settled the area, causing resentment among Palestinians. The Gaza Strip in the southwest includes the city of Gaza. This area gained a measure of self-rule in 1994. At present, the future of the "occupied territories" remains uncertain, although they have often been the subject of negotiation between Israel and its Arab neighbors and the Palestinians. The West Bank may one day become the basis for a new nation of Palestine, a homeland for the Palestinian Arabs.

The city of Jerusalem contains the most holy site of Judaism, the third holiest site of Islam, and the holiest site for Christians.

FACT FILE

- The highest point in Israel is Mount Meron, which is 3,963 feet (1,208 m) high, and the lowest is the Dead Sea shoreline, which is 1,312 feet (400 m) below sea level.

- Israel's longest river is the Jordan River at 205 miles (330 km) long.

- Israel's coastline is 170 miles (273 km) in length.

- The northernmost village of Metulla is about 280 miles (450 km) from Eilat in the south—nine hours journey by automobile. From east to west, Israel is never more than 110 miles (180 km) wide and only nine miles (15 km) across at its narrowest point.

TERRAIN

For such a small country, Israel has a very varied terrain. There are high, snow-dusted peaks, lush, subtropical valleys, green terraced hillsides, and dusty deserts. Israel also has two large lakes. In the north, Lake Kinneret is a deep freshwater lake also known as the Sea of Galilee or Lake Tiberias. In the east, the Dead Sea is a large lake that forms part of Israel's border with Jordan. Lying 1,312 feet (400 m) below sea level, it is the lowest-lying water surface on earth and the world's saltiest lake.

Israel's highest point (excluding the occupied territories) is Mount Meron, which rises to 3,963 feet (1,208 m) in the northern hills. The country's higher land is located toward the center, around Hebron and Jerusalem, and in the northern Golan Heights.

ISRAEL'S LANDFORMS

● **Coastal Plain**

This strip of land that runs along the Mediterranean coast is the most fertile area in Israel. As a result, most of the people, business, and farming are located in this region. Haifa, Israel's main port, is in the north of the strip and Tel Aviv is farther south. The coastal plain includes the Plain of Esdraelon and the Plain of Sharon, where citrus fruit is grown.

● **Judeo-Galilean Highlands**

The region includes a series of mountain ranges that run south from Galilee to the Negev Desert. The country's highest mountain, Mount Meron, is located in the region. Some agriculture takes place on the hills around Jerusalem, but the land to the south is suitable only for grazing livestock.

● **Negev Desert**

This is the driest region of Israel and is sparsely populated. The land has traditionally been used for grazing rather than growing crops but modern irrigation projects, using water from Lake Kinneret, have enabled parts of the desert to be cultivated.

● **Rift Valley**

The Rift Valley (see p. 20) is a narrow strip of land in the east of Israel. The part in Israel makes up only a fraction of the Great Rift Valley, which runs from Syria to Mozambique. The floor of the valley is flat, but it is bordered by steep sides. Most of the valley is below sea level and it includes the lowest land area on earth, the shore of the Dead Sea.

~ISRAEL~

Mediterranean Sea

LEBANON

SYRIA

Hula Valley

GOLAN HEIGHTS

Mt. Meron ▲

Nahariyya ●
Akko ●
Galilee
Tiberias ●
Haifa ◪
Lake Kinneret
Nazareth ●
Mt. Tabor ▲
Mt. Carmel ▲
Plain of Esdraelon
Qishon River
Hills of Samaria
Mt. Gilboa ▲

Caesarea ●
Hadera ●

Netanya ○
Plain of Sharon
Nablus ○
WEST BANK
Herziliyya ●
Yarkon River
Samaria
Jordan River

Tel Aviv-Jaffa ◪

Rehovot ●
Ramallah ●
Jericho ●

JERUSALEM ▫
Ashdod ○
Bethlehem ●
Ashkelon ●

Hebron ○
GAZA
Gaza City ◪
Hills of Judaea
Dead Sea
Ein Gedi ●

Beersheba ○
Dimona ●
JORDAN

Avdat ●
Negev Desert

EGYPT
Ramon Crater
Mt. Ramon ▲

Sinai Desert

N

Eilat ●
Gulf of Aqaba

Red Sea

KEY

Cities and towns by population

▫ over 500,000

◪ over 200,000

○ over 100,000

● under 100,000

Other symbols

▲ high points

- - - country border

Scale:
0 – 20 – 40 – 60 – 80 miles
0 – 30 – 60 – 90 – 120 km

REGIONS OF ISRAEL

Geographers usually divide Israel into five main regions. They are the coastal strip in the west, the Hills of Galilee in the north, the Samarian and Judaean Hills in the center, the Rift Valley in the east, and the Negev Desert in the south.

The Coastal Strip

The coastal strip is a narrow strip of land running along the eastern shore of the Mediterranean. This low-lying

area is watered by its many small rivers that flow down from the highlands in the center of Israel. In a land where water is scarce, the rivers make this one of Israel's main farming areas. Crops grown here include oranges, lemons, mangoes, grapefruit, tomatoes, strawberries, and avocados.

The coastal strip is Israel's most developed region. Two-thirds of the country's population lives there. It is also the most heavily industrialized area.

The Carmel Heights, near Haifa, are known as Little Switzerland and are home to much of Israel's wine industry.

The North

The Plain of Esdraelon lies in the north. It is separated from the rest of the lowlands by a ridge of high ground that rises to Mount Carmel near the coast. The plain is watered by the Quishon River. The town of Haifa grew up in the 20th century around a sheltered bay near the mouth of the river and spread up the slopes of Mount Carmel. Now Israel's third-largest city, it is a center for the oil and chemical industries, and the country's main port.

DISTRICTS OF ISRAEL

Occupied territories

Golan Heights

NORTHERN

Haifa

Nazareth

CENTRAL

Tel Aviv

West Bank

Ramla

JERUSALEM

Gaza Strip

Beersheba

SOUTHERN

Israel is divided into six districts: Central, Northern, Southern, Jerusalem, Tel Aviv, and Haifa. They are listed below with their capitals. These districts are further divided to create 15 subdistricts. Each district has its own government with its own budget, but the laws and budget are closely controlled by the central government.

CENTRAL Ramla
JERUSALEM Jerusalem
TEL AVIV Tel Aviv
HAIFA Haifa
SOUTHERN Beersheba
NORTHERN Nazareth

North of Haifa, Akko (Acre) is an ancient port with a Crusader fortress. To the south, Caesarea is one of Israel's most-visited ancient sites, with a Roman amphitheater and a Crusader castle. Close by, the town of Netanya is a popular beach resort and the center of Israel's diamond cutting industry.

In the north, the coastal strip is narrow—only about 10 miles (16 km) wide. Farther south, it broadens to a band of lowlands 25 miles (40 km) wide. The Plain of Sharon is a fertile farmland noted for its orange and lemon orchards. South of Netanya, Tel Aviv-Jaffa is Israel's second-largest city and the country's industry and business capital. Once this urban area was two separate cities, but the town of Tel Aviv grew so fast it merged with its neighbor, the ancient port of Jaffa. South of Tel Aviv lie the busy port of Ashdod and the ancient Philistine city of Ashkelon. Beyond these lies the Gaza Strip.

Originally a small Phoenician fishing village, Caesarea was developed by the Roman ruler Herod in about 22 B.C. It is now one of Israel's main archaeological sites.

The Hills of Galilee

The Hills of Galilee lie in northern Israel. In the far north near the border with Lebanon, the rugged mountains of Upper Galilee were formed by volcanic eruptions. The lava ejected from these ancient volcanoes hardened to form a tough, black rock called basalt. Mount Meron, Israel's highest mountain, lies in Upper Galilee. Farther south, the limestone hills of Lower Galilee are lower, rolling uplands cut by fertile valleys. To the east, the hills drop steeply down to the shores of Lake Kinneret. To the south, fertile valleys cut through the mountains. Nearby stands Mount Tabor, at 1,929 feet (588 m) the highest peak in the region.

The Hills of Galilee are home to most of Israel's Arab population. The village of Nazareth, where Jesus Christ is said to have grown up, is now a large Arab town. Christians visit the Basilica of the Annunciation, the church that marks the place where Christians believe the Angel Gabriel told Mary that she would bear a child who was the son of God.

The Samarian and Judaean Hills

Nazareth (An-Nasra) has a population that is half Muslim, half Christian. Upper Nazareth is a new Jewish industrial town.

The chains of mountains that lie in the center of Israel are known as the Samarian and Judaean Hills. Much of this highland region lies in the Israeli-occupied West Bank. The Samarian Hills in the north hold the West Bank towns of Nablus and Jericho. Jericho is a very ancient settlement with a history that stretches back many thousands of years (*see* pp. 44–45).

The city of Jerusalem, Israel's capital, stands at 2,400 feet (730 m) above sea level in the Judaean Hills. Farmers grow crops on the terraced hillsides (structured with banks or ridges) that stand around the city. To the east, the rocky Judaean Desert drops down to the Dead Sea. To the south, the hills become more rugged and less suitable for farming. Herds of sheep and goats graze the hillsides that stretch toward the barren Negev Desert.

The region of Judaea includes the West Bank towns of Hebron and Bethlehem. Hebron is an ancient city where Jews, Christians, and Muslims believe Abraham, the father of the Hebrew people, lies buried. Bethlehem is a popular place of pilgrimage for both Jews and Christians. Jews pay homage at David's Well, named after the ancient king of the Israelites who was born in the town. Christians worship at the Cave of the Nativity in Manger Square, traditionally the site where Christ was born.

Tensions between the Arab population of Hebron and Jewish settlers have led to violent confrontations and the posting of 2,500 Israeli soldiers in the town to prevent further bloodshed.

The Formation of the Rift Valley

1 The earth's crust is cracked where two plates meet.

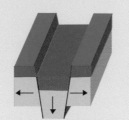

2 The two plates pull apart, creating a steep-sided trench.

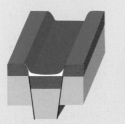

3 The sharp trench edges are rounded by erosion.

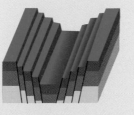

4 Parallel faults in the trench wall create a valley.

The Great Rift Valley was formed by an upheaval in the earth's crust millions of years ago. Geologists know that the earth's outer crust is not one solid layer. Instead, the land and oceans rest on a number of huge plates that fit together like pieces of a giant jigsaw.

Millions of years ago, the Rift Valley area lay on a fault line—a crack in the earth's crust where two plates met (*see* 1 above). Over a huge span of time, the two plates slowly pulled apart (2), causing volcanic activity and earthquakes. Eventually, a wide valley formed, flanked by high ground with volcanoes (3–4). Water heated by volcanic activity underground forced its way to the surface in the region, forming hot springs. The springs at Lake Kinneret and the Dead Sea contain minerals believed to cure many illnesses.

The Rift Valley

The Rift Valley forms a long, narrow strip along Israel's eastern border. It is part of the great Rift Valley system that runs south from Syria through the Middle East and down through East Africa as far as Mozambique. Geological upheaval created this giant, steep-sided, flat-bottomed valley millions of years ago.

The Syrian–African Rift Valley system that runs through Israel from north to south is one of the earth's most prominent natural features. Stretching for a total of 4,000 miles (6,500 km), this striking feature is so large that it can be seen from space.

From its source to the north, the Jordan River flows through the fertile Hula Valley. This region was a swampy marshland before it was drained in the 1950s. Now Hula is rich farming country noted for its orchards and cotton fields. To the east, the Hula Valley is overlooked by the Golan Heights. Just north of the Golan Heights, in Syria, the land rises to the highest peak in the region, Mount

Hebron, 9,230 feet (2,814 m). The peaks of the mountain are snow-covered all year round.

South of the Hula Valley, the Jordan flows into Lake Kinneret. Measuring 13 miles (21 km) by seven miles (11 km), this deep lake is Israel's most important source of freshwater. The lake's Hebrew name comes from its shape, which is said to resemble a harp (*kinnor* in Hebrew). As the Sea of Galilee, the lake is mentioned in the New Testament. Jesus' disciples, Peter and his brother Andrew, were fishermen who lived by its shore.

The Jordan River

The Jordan flows through the northern part of the Rift Valley. It holds great significance for Christians as the river in which Jesus was baptized. The Jordan is Israel's longest river, flowing for a total of 205 miles (330 km). It rises in the far north, fed by streams that gush down from the high mountains of neighboring Syria. From its source, it flows south along the Rift Valley to empty into the Dead Sea via Lake Kinneret.

Hymns and folk songs sung around the world describe the Jordan as "deep and wide." In fact, the river flows strongly only in the north. As it nears the end of its course, the great heat of the Rift Valley causes much of the water to evaporate. Only a trickle reaches the Dead Sea.

The Dead Sea

Even nonswimmers find they cannot sink in the Dead Sea. The water has the greatest concentration of salt of any lake in the world. In fact, a glass of Dead Sea water contains about one-third salt. Minerals makes the lake's water so buoyant that it is difficult to dive beneath the surface. Swimmers can read a newspaper while floating on their backs without getting the pages wet.

The southern section of the Dead Sea is the saltiest. There the salt has hardened to make strange rock formations shaped like turrets and mushrooms. The waters of the Dead Sea contain other minerals too, including bromine, magnesium, potassium, and iodine. These valuable minerals are harvested for industry.

The Dead Sea is actually a lake lying at the mouth of the Jordan River. It forms part of Israel's border with Jordan and its shore is the lowest place on the surface of the earth. The reason the lake is called the Dead Sea is because no fish except brine shrimp and very few plants are able to survive in its salty waters.

The lake covers about 400 sq. miles (1,036 sq. km) and is about 50 miles (80 km) long. The lake is deepest in the north, where the bed lies some 1,300 feet (400 m) below the surface and almost 2,625 feet (800 m) below sea level. However, since the early 1900s the lake's water level has been falling steadily due to lack of rain. The lake has been depleted by water drawn off for irrigation from its source, the freshwater Jordan River.

The deep waters of Lake Kinneret contain many kinds of fish, including one known as St. Peter's fish. Today people visit the lake to camp and picnic on its beaches. Vacationers windsurf and water-ski on the lake, or sample St. Peter's fish in the restaurants that line the shore.

Tiberias is the largest town on the shores of Lake Kinneret. It was founded by King Herod the Great (*see* p. 54), who ruled Palestine in Roman times, 2,000 years ago. Beyond Lake Kinneret, the Jordan continues south along the Rift Valley to drain into the Dead Sea. The properties of this large lake have been noted since ancient times and chemicals from its waters were sold to the ancient Egyptians for use in embalming.

The ancient settlement of Qumran lies in the West Bank territory in the cliffs above the Dead Sea. The site

Lake Kinneret has been settled since prehistoric times. The oldest find on the lake's shores, the skull of a man, dates to the Paleolithic era, around 100,000 B.C.

Masada

Masada is an ancient fortress on a mountain on the shores of the Dead Sea. It was built by Herod the Great 2,000 years ago. The fortress included a palace, defense towers, and large water cisterns (basins) cut into the rock. In A.D. 66, a group of 1,000 Jewish rebels took refuge in the fortress during a revolt against the Romans. The Romans laid siege to Masada with 15,000 men. When defeat became inevitable, the Jewish rebels inside committed suicide rather than surrender. Today, the fortress is seen as a symbol of the heroic resistance of the Jewish people.

The Dead Sea Scrolls were the work of the Essenes, a Jewish sect who lived in seclusion at Qumran. The scrolls are now in the Israel Museum in Jerusalem.

became famous when, in 1947, a bedouin shepherd boy stumbled upon an archive of ancient texts known as the Dead Sea Scrolls in a cave there. These included versions of books of the Bible and other religious texts.

The Jordan River stops at the Dead Sea. The intense heat of the Rift Valley causes water to evaporate from the lake and hang in a mist above it. So much moisture evaporates that the water level in the lake remains constant.

Beyond the Dead Sea, the Rift Valley runs through a long, narrow strip of low-lying desert called the Arava. From this depression, the rift heads south to meet the deep waters of the Red Sea at the Gulf of Aqaba.

The Negev Desert

The Negev Desert is an important strategic area for Israel and the government has done much to encourage settlement there.

The Negev is a triangle of land that forms the southern part of Israel. The region covers over half of Israel, yet only 10 percent of the population lives there because the climate is so dry. In the north of the Negev, where it is broadest, the ground is covered by a powdery yellow

soil called loess, which is very fertile when watered. Large areas of the northern desert have now been irrigated and turned into farmland.

The city of Beersheba in the north of the Negev is the largest town in the region. Jews believe the city was founded by Abraham, mentioned in the Bible as the father of the Jewish people. The city is now the site of a major bedouin market, where traditional goods such as carpets and pottery are sold. Forty miles (65 km) south of Beersheba lies an ancient city called Avdat. It was built by a people called the Nabataeans over 2,000 years ago. The Nabataeans were skilled engineers and builders. They cut deep channels in the rock to funnel water into giant rock-cut cisterns (basins). In this way, they could conserve scarce supplies of water and turn the area around Avdat into a green desert oasis.

The southern part of the Negev is even drier and more barren than the northern part of the desert. The stony and sandy desert is cut by dry riverbeds called wadis. Only after occasional rainstorms do these rocky channels fill with water. Few people live in the southern Negev, but tourists visit the area to see the spectacular desert scenery. They marvel at the towering sandstone cliffs, bare rocky peaks, and the world's three largest craters. The Ramon Crater, 25 miles (40 km) across, is the largest crater in the world.

In the far south, the town of Eilat lies on the Gulf of Aqaba. Eilat is both a busy port and a popular tourist destination. Vacationers enjoy the clear blue waters of the Gulf and its sandy beaches. Divers explore the undersea world of the coral reefs that teem with colorful fish.

Eilat

The ancient city of Eilat is referred to several times in the Bible and has been a traditional refuge for Jews fleeing persecution. It is Israel's only Red Sea port, and thus its only link with the Indian Ocean and East Asia. The city's strategic location has long made it a point of contention between Israel and its Arab neighbors. In order to ensure that Eilat was safeguarded, the Israeli government was keen to ensure that it was well populated. It offered generous incentives to anyone who was prepared to settle there. As a result, Eilat's population has increased rapidly in recent years.

The Bedouin

The bedouin are an Arabic-speaking nomadic people who traditionally have inhabited Middle Eastern deserts, especially in Arabia, Iraq, Syria, and Jordan. However, some bedouin groups have migrated into the Negev Desert region of Israel. Today there are around 60,000 bedouin living in Israel.

The bedouin fall into two basic classes: those who live a nomadic life herding livestock, and a newer group who have a more settled lifestyle, such as those below, living on the edge of the desert, where they grow their own food.

The nomadic bedouin use camels for transportation in the desert. These "ships of the desert" are highly valued in bedouin society and a man's wealth is partly assessed by how many camels he owns. The nomads live in portable black tents made from goat's hair. The tents are divided into two. One half is used by the women and children for cooking and storage, while the other half will usually have a fire and be used for entertainment and socializing. The women do most of the domestic work in the society, while the men plan the group's movements.

Sheep and goats are important to the survival of the bedouin but in recent years some nomads have taken manual labor jobs in order to earn money. However, most bedouin still regard this type of work as degrading.

CLIMATE

In general terms, Israel has a Mediterranean climate. This means that summers are long, hot, and dry, and winters are cool, mild, and rainy. The changes between the seasons are less noticeable than they are in northern Europe and most of North America. All parts of Israel have many days of sunshine. However, the climate varies in different areas.

The north of Israel is generally cooler than the southern part. The climate also depends on how high the land is and how close to the sea. Hills and mountains are generally cooler than low-lying regions. The Rift Valley region, where the land is below sea level, is, however, very hot. Inland areas experience greater variations in temperature than places near the coast, where the sea has a moderating influence on the climate.

Differences in climate are marked between Eilat in the southern desert and Jerusalem in the hilly center of the country.

Winter (November to February) is the main rainy season in Israel. The rainiest month is December. No rain falls from May to October. However, rain does not fall evenly throughout the country. The north and west are much wetter than the south and east. The Hills of Galilee in the northwest are the wettest area of all, receiving 42 inches (108 cm) of rain each year. The city of Jerusalem in the Judaean Hills gets 22 inches (55 cm)—surprisingly, about the same amount as London, England. The Negev Desert in southern Israel gets very little rain. The driest parts of the Negev receive less than 10 inches (25 cm) of rain a year.

January is the coldest month in Israel, but even this is still comparatively mild. The average winter

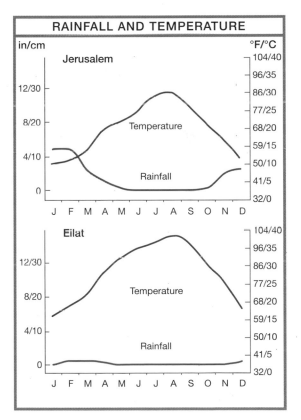

RAINFALL AND TEMPERATURE

Jerusalem

Eilat

temperature in Tel Aviv is 57°F (14°C). In Jerusalem it is cooler—with an average temperature of 48°F (9°C). Many winter days are clear and sunny, but a cloudburst may bring as much as four inches (10 cm) of rain in a single day. Snow hardly ever falls on the coastal plain. In the hills of Jerusalem there may be one or two days of snow each year. On these rare days, busloads of excited children arrive from the south to enjoy the snow.

Soil erosion in Israel has led to frequent flooding in some areas. The government is trying to solve this problem by planting a large number of trees, the roots of which hold the soil in place.

Although southern Israel generally receives much less rain in winter, occasional rainstorms fill dry riverbeds with surging water, causing dangerous flash floods. Temperatures in the south remain warm all year. In Eilat on the Red Sea, daytime winter temperatures rarely drop below 68°F (20°C).

After the winter rains, the north and central hills are green in spring. As summer advances, the earth becomes brown and parched. August is the hottest month. In Tel Aviv the average temperature rises to 81°F (27°C). The coastal plain is humid, hot, and sticky. Temperatures soar in the Rift Valley. Up in the hills, Jerusalem is cooler, with an average of 75°F (24°C). Eilat in the far south regularly bakes in summer temperatures of 104°F (40°C).

In spring and again in autumn, many parts of Israel are plagued by a hot, dry wind that blows in from the Arabian Desert to the east. This seasonal wind, called the *sharav* in Hebrew and the *khamsin* in Arabic, sends temperatures soaring with a hot desert air that blows gritty sand everywhere.

WILDLIFE AND PLANTS

Israel is home to a wide range of plants and animals. With a land area one-sixth the size of England, the country is home to over 2,500 different species of plants, compared to England's 1,700. The key to this diversity is Israel's location, on a land bridge linking Asia and Africa. The different climate zones within the country support different communities of wildlife.

In the west, the coastal plain was once covered with dense forest and scrub (an area of stunted trees and shrubs). Over the centuries most of the forests were cut down, but recently, thanks to a program of replanting, the forests are returning. In spring, the Hills of Galilee in the north are bright with poppies and anemones.

In the east, the Rift Valley and Judaean Desert are too dry for most plants. The vegetation is mainly low bush and scrub. At Jericho and Ein Gedi in the West Bank, springs bubble to the surface to create green oases where subtropical plants bloom. The lotus tree, giant

The Society for the Protection of Nature in Israel has a network of field study centers around the country involved in research and conservation.

Date palms flourish in an oasis of the Negev Desert.

reed, Christ's thorn, and Sodom apple are some of the rare plants that flourish at Ein Gedi.

The Negev Desert is home to plants that can survive for long periods with very little water. Many trees and plants that grow there have long roots that spread far underground to suck up every last drop of moisture. Their small or waxy leaves help keep moisture in. Sharp thorns, thick bark, or bitter sap keep hungry animals at bay.

Few plants can survive in the stoniest parts of the Negev, but thorn shrubs grow along the wadis (dry valleys). When storm clouds gather and rain falls at last, seeds that have lain in the soil for months, even years, germinate and sprout quickly. Plants flower, set seed, and wither again all in a matter of a few days. Weeks later, the same area of desert looks bare and lifeless once more.

The Land of Milk and Honey

In biblical times Israel was known as "the land of milk and honey."

Desert plants like this vetch have small leaves to conserve water and sharp spines to deter predators.

The Bible describes lush vineyards, fields of waving corn, and oak forests covering much of northern and central Israel. Now much of the same region is dry and barren. Scientists believe the felling of Israel's forests caused the transformation. Without tree roots to anchor the earth, fertile soil washed away. Herds of sheep and goats overgrazed the grassy hillsides, causing more erosion. Gradually, the soil in many parts became barren and lacking in nutrients, fit only to support thorny scrub. In modern times, barren areas have been irrigated to become fertile once again.

Replanting Israel's Forests

In ancient times, much of Israel was covered with dense forests of oak, pine, and terebinth (a small tree that produces turpentine). Over the centuries, as successive empires conquered Palestine, the forests were cut down by armies seeking fuel and timber for weapons. Farmers and herders also cut down trees to create new fields and pastures. During World War I (1914–1918), Turkish soldiers felled some of Israel's last forests to build a railroad to the Arabian Desert.

The 20th century saw a massive program of tree planting in Israel. An organization called the Jewish National Fund (JNF) coordinated much of the planting. Since 1948, a remarkable 200 million trees have been planted. Now young forests of pine, cypress, oak, and eucalyptus flourish. Four million new trees are currently planted every year.

Tu B'Shevat, National Arbor Day, falls on the 15th day of the Jewish month of Shevat. Children and adults plant saplings and return each year to check on their growth. Trees are also planted to mark birthdays and weddings. Today forests again cover 770 square miles (2,000 sq. km) of Israel—10 percent of the total land area. Tree roots help to stabilize the ground to prevent soil erosion, and provide habitats for animals and birds.

Animals

Israel is home to over 70 different kinds of mammals. In ancient times, lions, tigers, bears, and ostriches were all found there. Over the centuries, these animals were hunted to extinction, along with several kinds of antelope. Leopards were also thought to be extinct, but they were recently discovered living near the oasis of Ein Gedi in the Judaean Desert. Wolves, jackals, foxes, and hyenas all roam wild, as well as smaller mammals such as hedgehogs, porcupines, rock hyraxes, and leaping rodents called jerboas. Antelope and ibex, a type of large wild goat, graze the rocky uplands. Wild boar, water buffalo, and otter live in the northern woods.

Over 380 different kinds of birds can be seen in Israel. Some live there all year round. Eagles, vultures, and hawks nest on rocky cliffs. Ravens and birds called coursers live in the desert. Gulls and waterfowl are found by ponds or on the coast. Many other species

Israel is the second-largest flyway for birds after South America. The country is the southern limit for many northern bird species and the northern limit for many southern species.

A caracal, one of the large cats that inhabit the Negev Desert.

Due to the depletion of many of Israel's natural water sources and fish stocks, fish are now farmed in cages. Many of these are located off the Red Sea coast and in Lake Kinneret.

visit Israel during migration. Storks, pelicans, and birds of prey pass through as they fly south in fall on their way to Africa, and north again in spring.

Israel has 80 species of reptiles, including seven kinds of tortoise. Snakes include the poisonous Palestinian viper; lizards include geckos and chameleons. Crocodiles once lived along a river near Haifa, but they have died out in the wild and are now only seen on crocodile farms.

Israel's seas and inland waters contain many different species of fish. Bass, bream, mullet, hake, sharks, rays, and shellfish are all found in the Mediterranean waters off Israel's coast. The coral reefs of the Red Sea attract bright tropical fish including butterflyfish and cowfish. The many different types of coral also support a huge variety of other marine life, including crustaceans, sponges, eels, and turtles.

National Parks and Conservation

Israel's 280 national parks and nature reserves together cover 1,540 square miles (400 sq km)—more than 20 percent of the whole country. Some major reserves are shown on the map on the right. These protected sites are home to rare plants or animals, or preserve unusual landscapes. They are administered by the National Reserves Authority. Some offer tourist facilities or networks of hiking trails. Others are off-limits to the general public. All visitors to the national parks must follow strict guidelines aimed at preserving their natural beauty. Another conservation organization, the Society for the Protection of Nature in Israel, has 24 field schools scattered throughout Israel. Guests stay to learn about conservation.

Two of the most famous reserves in Israel are Banias in the Golan Heights in the north, and Ein Gedi near the Dead Sea. Wild cats, stone martens, and otters are among the alpine species found at Banias. The park also contains the remains of an ancient temple and a Crusader fort. Ein Gedi is home to leopards, ibex, and rock hyraxes.

The 1960s saw the start of an exciting wildlife program called Hai-Bar in Israel. It aims to reintroduce species mentioned in the Bible that have since become extinct. Thanks to Hai-Bar, ostriches, wild asses, and addax and oryx antelopes now roam again in Israel. The program has several reserves, including one on Mount Carmel, and another, the Hai Bar Reserve, in the Arava Desert, north of Eilat.

ISRAEL'S CITIES

Over 90 percent of Israel's population live in urban areas. These are concentrated on the western coastline. To a large extent this is due to the development of the plains here. In addition to the major Jewish-dominated cities of Jerusalem, Tel Aviv, and Haifa, there are major Arab centers farther inland at Hebron, Ramallah, and Beersheba (*see* pp. 44–45).

JERUSALEM

Jerusalem is Israel's largest city and the nation's capital. It is one of the world's most famous cities. Jerusalem is divided into two parts: East and West Jerusalem. West Jerusalem is home to many Jews. It contains fine modern buildings and some ancient sites. Many Arabs live in East Jerusalem. The old city in East Jerusalem contains some of the world's most holy places.

In 1948, when Israel was set up, the United Nations gave it control of West Jerusalem. East Jerusalem was part of Jordan. During the Six-Day War in 1967 (*see* p.71), Israel seized East Jerusalem and made the whole city the capital of Israel. Today some countries do not recognize Jerusalem as Israel's capital because the United Nations wanted it to be an international city. The Palestinian Arabs also claim the city as their capital.

The Church of the Holy Sepulchre in Jerusalem, the most important site in Christendom, marks the spot where it is believed Christ was crucified.

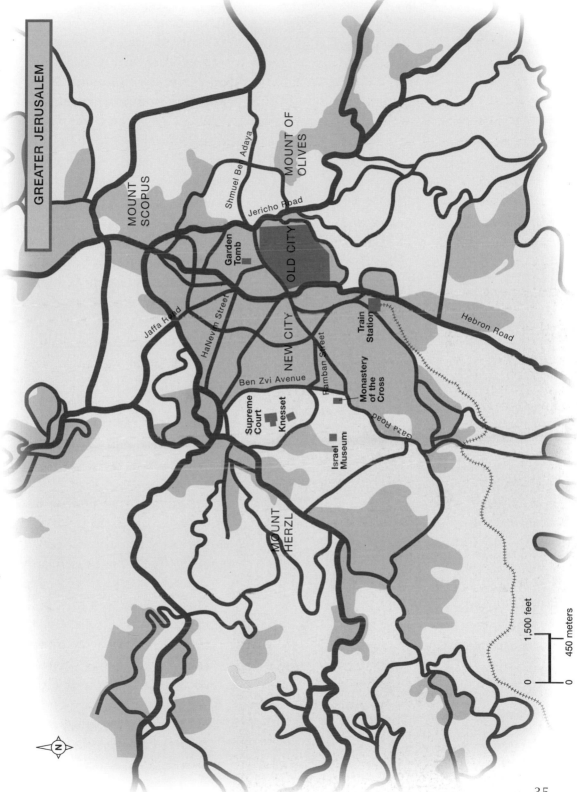

GREATER JERUSALEM

MOUNT OF OLIVES

MOUNT SCOPUS

Shmuel Ben Adaya

Jericho Road

Garden Tomb

OLD CITY

Jaffa Road

HaNevim Street

NEW CITY

Hebron Road

Train Station

Ramban Street

Ben Zvi Avenue

Monastery of the Cross

Gaza Road

Supreme Court

Knesset

Israel Museum

MOUNT HERZL

1,500 feet

450 meters

0

0

N

Orthodox Jews at the Western Wall in East Jerusalem, the last remaining part of the ancient temple building.

Jerusalem's History

Jerusalem is the spiritual center of the Jewish religion and an important center for Muslims and Christians. For 3,000 years, Jews have turned to face Jerusalem when they pray. The city first became capital of Israel under David, king of the Israelites, in around 1000 B.C. David's son, King Solomon, then built a magnificent temple in Jerusalem. When it was destroyed, a second temple was built in its place.

Over the centuries, many different empires have governed Israel from Jerusalem. Successive rulers built stout stone walls to defend the old city. The local honey-colored limestone, known as Jerusalem stone, was used to construct walls and buildings. The walls have been broken down and rebuilt about 20 times. Seven gates lead through the walls into the old city.

Sights of the Old City

Jerusalem's old city contains four historic districts, or quarters. They are the Muslim, Christian, Jewish, and Armenian quarters. Each quarter has its own historic buildings and markets. Many of the ancient cobbled streets are too narrow for automobiles, so heavy loads are delivered by camel or donkey.

Jerusalem is holy ground for three of the world's major religions: Judaism, Christianity, and Islam. For Jews,

OLD JERUSALEM

Damascus
Gate

MUSLIM QUARTER

Via Dolorosa

New
Gate

CHRISTIAN
QUARTER

Temple Mount

Dome of
the Rock

Church of the
Holy Sepulchre

Jaffa Gate

The
Citadel

Western
Wall

JEWISH QUARTER

ARMENIAN
QUARTER

N

the most sacred monument is the Western Wall. It is all
that remains of the second temple, built by Herod the
Great 2,000 years ago, but destroyed by the Romans in
A.D. 70. The Western Wall is also known as the Wailing
Wall, after the sorrowful sounds made by Jews during the
Ottoman period (*see* p. 63) mourning the destruction of
the temple. Every day, many Jews visit the Western Wall
to pray. Some press slips of paper with written prayers
into cracks in the wall.

Close to the Western Wall stands the Dome of the
Rock, the Muslim monument many people feel is
Jerusalem's most beautiful building. It was built about
1,300 years ago. The shining golden dome is a prominent landmark. The walls are covered with glazed tiles

The Dome of the Rock was built by Abd al-Malik, the Ummayad caliph in the seventh century. The brilliant mosaics on the exterior were renewed in 1963.

and intricate mosaics. It is believed that this is the place where Abraham offered to sacrifice his son Isaac, to prove his faith in God. Muslims believe the shrine marks the spot where the prophet Mohammed rose to heaven. Jerusalem is Islam's third most sacred city, after Mecca and Medina in Saudi Arabia.

Jerusalem is also a holy city for Christians because many important events in the life of Jesus Christ took place there. The Church of the Holy Sepulchre is believed to have been built on the Hill of Calvary where Jesus was crucified and later buried. The present-day church was built by Crusaders 950 years ago, on the site of an earlier church. A street called the Via Dolorosa (Way of Sorrows) leads east through the Muslim quarter to Gethsemane. Christians believe this was the route along which Christ carried his cross to Calvary. The 14 Stations of the Cross mark stages along this route, from the point where he was condemned to death to the site of his crucifixion and burial, both located within the Church of the Holy Sepulchre.

Modern Jerusalem

The city now extends far beyond the boundaries of old Jerusalem. The new city includes gleaming shopping malls, luxury hotels, and modern offices and factories, as well as many historic buildings. Israel's parliament building, the Knesset, is located near the center. Close by are the magnificent Israel Museum and the Shrine of the Book that houses the Dead Sea Scrolls, the Hebrew University, and the seventh-century Monastery of the Cross. The modern city contains few tall skyscrapers to mar the outlines of the old city. All new buildings are made from yellowish Jerusalem stone, which makes the whole city glow golden at sunset.

The Israel Museum houses a large collection of Jewish folk art and archaeological exhibits, including some of the Dead Sea Scrolls. Probably the most commonly visited museum is Yad Vashem, which commemorates the Holocaust (*see* p. 69). The Jewish National and University Library, which is located in the Hebrew University of Jerusalem holds 3.5 million volumes.

The diverse architecture of modern Jerusalem, including Italian, Russian, and colonial styles, reflects the make-up of early Jewish settlers.

The form of the Shrine of the Book at the Israel Museum is supposed to resemble the clay pots in which the Dead Sea Scrolls were found.

TEL AVIV–JAFFA

Tel Aviv is Israel's second-largest city, and the main center for industry and business. It lies close to the ancient port of Jaffa (Yafo) and officially merged with it in 1950. Greater Tel Aviv–Jaffa is home to nearly two million people—40 percent of Israel's population. This area includes a cluster of other large towns, including Petah Tikva, Rehovot, and Rishon Le Zion, which have sprung up on the plain around the city.

Tel Aviv is a new city—in fact, the first Jewish city built in the last two hundred years. It was founded in 1909 as a new suburb for Jaffa. But the new town grew rapidly and became Israel's most fashionable city. Now it is home to many of Israel's tallest buildings, with offices, shops, restaurants, nightclubs, dozens of museums and galleries, and many foreign embassies.

The skyline of Tel Aviv is dominated by its beachside hotels and by the towers of its banking district.

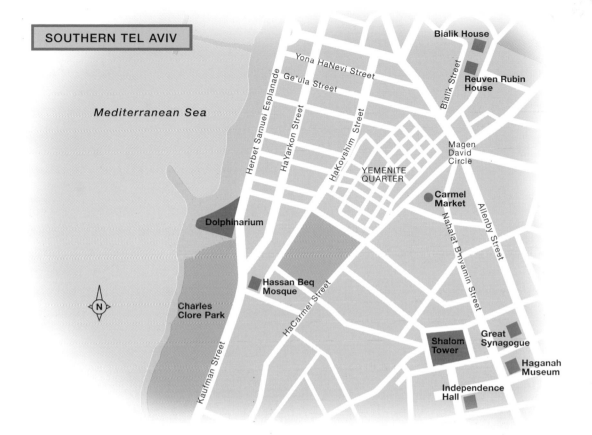

SOUTHERN TEL AVIV

Bialik House

Yona HaNevi Street

Ge'ula Street

Reuven Rubin House

Bialik Street

Herbet Samuel Esplanade

Mediterranean Sea

HaYarkon Street

Hakovshim Street

Magen David Circle

YEMENITE QUARTER

Carmel Market

Allenby Street

Dolphinarium

Nahalat B'nyamin Street

Hassan Beq Mosque

HaCarmel Street

Charles Clore Park

N

Kaufman Street

Shalom Tower

Great Synagogue

Haganah Museum

Independence Hall

The sights of Tel Aviv include Bialik Street, at the heart of the first Jewish district, built in the 1920s. There are also the busy Carmel Market and Ben-Gurion House, once the home of Israel's first prime minister. Popular attractions include the Eretz Israel (Land of Israel) Museum, a collection of 11 museums based around an archaeological site, and the Museum of the Diaspora, which tells the story of Jewish communities set up around the world. The Shalom Tower is a tall skyscraper which contains a wax museum displaying many figures from history. But Tel Aviv's main attractions are its beautiful white sandy beaches and warm climate. The seafront includes a vast range of hotels, a marina, a public swimming pool, and many lively cafés.

Important industries in Tel Aviv are diamond-cutting, publishing, and media. Tel Aviv is a major cultural center and is home to the Israel Philharmonic Orchestra

Modernist Architecture

In the 1930s, persecution in Germany meant that many Jews fled to Tel Aviv. They brought with them a minimalist, functional style of architecture known as Modernism, particularly that associated with the German Bauhaus movement. After the destruction of many buildings in Germany during World War II, Tel Aviv is one of the few remaining centers of such Modernist architecture.

About 1,500 buildings are marked for preservation, but as no public funds are currently available, private funds must ensure the buildings' survival.

and a number of theatrical companies. Tel Aviv University (founded 1953) and Bar-Ilan University (1955) are important centers of learning.

Tel Aviv's History

In 1909 the city of Tel Aviv began as a Jewish settlement on a sand dune north of Jaffa and, like Israel, it has had a troubled history. During World War I, Jewish settlers were expelled by the Turks, who governed the area of Palestine at the time (*see* p. 66), because of their support for the Allies fighting against Germany and Turkey. Jewish settlers returned to Israel after the British took control of Palestine in 1917. Four years later, the native Arabs rioted against Jewish settlers who had emigrated to Tel Aviv, swelling its numbers. During the Nazi persecution of the Jews in Europe in the 1930s, Tel Aviv's population leapt dramatically from 45,000 to 145,000 due to the influx of European refugees.

When Israel achieved independence in 1948, Tel Aviv became the temporary capital of the country and was bombed repeatedly by Egyptian aircraft. In 1949, the capital was moved to Jerusalem. Tel Aviv and Jaffa were brought together as a single city in 1950, and this sprawling urban area grew rapidly in the 1950s when Jewish survivors of the Holocaust in World War II (*see* p. 69) poured in from Europe. During the Persian Gulf War in 1991, Tel Aviv was the main target of Scud missiles launched from Iraq, despite the fact that Israel did not take part in the war. The entire population of the city was provided with gas masks in case the Scuds were carrying chemical weapons, and was defended by advanced missile detection systems.

Jaffa

Just south of Tel Aviv, Jaffa is one of the world's oldest ports. The Bible tells how the prophet Jonah sailed from here, only to be swallowed by a whale during a storm. Over the centuries, Jaffa passed through the hands of many conquerors. The port is still busy. Much of Israel's citrus crop leaves the country from here, including the world-famous Jaffa oranges. For visitors, the sights of Jaffa include the old port and lighthouse, the clocktower, a scattering of mosques, Christian churches and monasteries, the flea market, and the old Turkish bathhouse.

The site of Jaffa has been populated for nearly 4,000 years. In ancient times, the Egyptians, Persians, and Greeks besieged the town, and remains of all three great empires have been found at the port. Jaffa was destroyed by the Romans during the war against the Jews in A.D. 68. The town was captured by the Christian Crusaders twice during the 12th century, only to be retaken by Muslim forces on each occasion. In the 19th century the influx of Jewish settlers caused tensions with the local Arab population. Later, in 1921, these overflowed into full-fledged riots against the Jews. In 1948, when the port was recaptured by Jewish forces, most of the people already living there—largely Arabs—were forced to flee.

Today the town, overshadowed by neighboring Tel Aviv, is largely a tourist attraction and its Arab architecture has been renovated to create a pleasant, if somewhat bland, town center. Attempts have also been made to create an artists' community in the town.

Towns of the West Bank

The West Bank is a much-disputed territory that lies between Israel and Jordan. It is about 2,260 square miles (5,860 sq. km) and has a population of around 1.5 million people, most of whom are Arabs. Historically, the area was part of Palestine, but it was annexed by Jordan in 1950. In 1967 Israel captured the West Bank but agreed to begin withdrawal in 1994.

Bethlehem

Bethlehem lies six miles (ten km) south of Jerusalem and has a population of just over 20,000. In Hebrew the name Bethlehem means "house of bread" or "house of Lahm" (a god).

It is known throughout the Christian world as the birthplace of Jesus Christ. The Church of the Nativity stands on the spot where he is thought to have been born.

Bethlehem is an important town for Jewish people as well. It was here that Rachel, one of the ancient ancestors of the Hebrews, died, and the town was the birthplace of David, king of Israel.

Over the years, the town has changed hands many times. Romans, Byzantines, Crusaders, Turks, and the British have all at one time ruled Bethlehem. Today it is the Palestinians who control the town.

The ancient town of Bethlehem, south of Jerusalem, seen from the hills.

Hebron

Hebron is an administrative and market center in the West Bank. Its major industries include glass-making, tanning, and food-processing. There are also stone and marble quarries. It has a population of around 100,000.

Hebron is one of the world's oldest cities. It is mentioned in the book of Genesis in the Bible and is of religious importance to Christians, Jews, and Muslims. The reason for its religious significance is the Cave of Machpelah. It was here that Abraham, ancestor of the Hebrews, is thought to be buried. Today, a mosque has been built on the site to which all visitors are admitted.

Jews were driven out of the city in the early 20th century, but in 1972 some Jews began settling on the edge of the town. Slowly, they began to move back into the center of the city and took possession of a street located in the former Jewish quarter. Today, there is tension between the Jewish and Muslim inhabitants of Hebron, and the Jewish street is guarded by Israeli soldiers and police. There are a number of concrete barricades and road blocks around the city.

Jericho

Jericho claims to be the world's oldest town and many scholars believe that it was settled as early as 8000 B.C. Jericho can certainly claim to be the world's lowest town, at 820 feet (250 m) below

sea-level. Jericho is probably best known for the story in the book of Joshua in the Bible, telling how the walls of the town crumbled at the sound of the Israelites' trumpets.

Jericho is an oasis town and, in contrast to its desert surroundings, enjoys lush vegetation supported by its underground water supply. During the winter, its 10,000 inhabitants have warm and pleasant weather compared to Jerusalem. Tourists are attracted by ancient palaces and synagogues as well as the chance to see the excavation of ancient Jericho. Nearby is the famous Mount of Temptation, where according to Matthew's gospel, Jesus was tempted by the Devil to convert stones into bread.

Past and Present

"Pessimism is a luxury that a Jew never can allow himself."

Former prime minister of Israel Golda Meir

The modern nation of Israel has existed for little more than 50 years. But the land has a much older history, which stretches back many thousands of years. For centuries, the early history of Israel was known through the books of the Bible. More recently the religious importance of the country led Israel to become a major region for archaeological excavation. Some of the new discoveries produced during this work have offered similar histories to those in the Bible, others have added to our knowledge of the period.

Over the centuries, many empires have conquered and occupied the region, among them the Egyptians, the Babylonians, the Persians, the Arabian empires, the Turkish Ottoman empire, and finally the British empire. Throughout this turbulent history, many different people have lived in the land now occupied by modern Israel. During the Roman occupation, which began in 63 B.C., the Jews were exiled or forced to flee from the region. They set up communities in many different countries around the world, but always thought of Israel as their spiritual home.

Jews began to resettle in the region in the 19th century, living beside the Arabs who settled in the area over a thousand years ago. Both Jews and Arabs now claim a historic right to areas in Israel and to an extent the modern history of Israel has been the history of these claims.

Crowds of Jewish children wave Israeli flags, celebrating Independence Day near the Western Wall in East Jerusalem.

FACT FILE

● The Jewish festival of Passover (Pesah) celebrates the ancient Israelites' delivery from slavery in Egypt.

● After the Diaspora, Hebrew gradually became disused as a living language. It was revived by the scholar Eliezer Ben-Yehuda, who emigrated to Israel in the 1880s.

● In 1979, Egypt's president, Anwar al-Sadat, and Israel's prime minister, Menachem Begin, were jointly awarded the Nobel Peace Prize for helping to advance peace in the Middle East. In 1981, Sadat was assassinated by an Islamic fundamentalist.

JERICHO

In prehistoric times, Israel was home to one of the world's earliest civilizations. At Jericho in the Judaean Desert, archaeologists have found the remains of a fortified city that is believed to date back to 8000 B.C. The ruins include stout stone walls and a tall defensive tower. Jericho must have been one of the earliest places where people abandoned a wandering life of hunting animals and gathering plants, and settled down to farm. At Jericho, finds such as cowrie shells from the Red Sea and turquoise from Sinai show that the townspeople traded with distant regions.

As the centuries passed at Jericho, successive generations built new cities on the crumbled ruins of the old ones. The remains built up to form a giant mound which is called a tell. Archaeologists have dug deep into the tell at Jericho to uncover the earliest remains at the bottom. Digs at other sites in Israel show that early people also settled along the Mediterranean, in the Jordan Valley, and the Negev.

Excavations at Jericho have uncovered layer after layer of remains from thousands of years of history.

Archaeologists base what they know of the distant past on excavations of old sites and also on ancient writings. Writing was invented in the Middle East around 3000 B.C. For Israel's ancient history, we have a rich source of information in the first five books of the Bible. Known in the Jewish tradition as the Torah, these books were probably written before 700 B.C. Archaeological finds bear out many of the historical details they contain.

Around 3000 B.C., the land that is now Israel was inhabited by a people called the Canaanites. Different groups of Canaanites built city kingdoms throughout the land. The superpowers of the time were Egypt and Assyria, the latter lay in Mesopotamia to the northeast of modern Israel. Land routes between the two empires ran through the land of Canaan.

THE ANCIENT HEBREWS

Between 1800 and 1500 B.C., a Semitic people (a racial group from southwestern Asia) from Mesopotamia moved to Canaan. They were the Hebrews, the ancestors of the Jewish people, and their patriarch, or leader, was named Abraham. The Bible tells how Abraham journeyed across the desert, then pitched his tent and settled at Beersheba. He, his son Isaac, and his grandson Jacob worshiped one god whom they called Yahweh, in a land where other peoples had many gods. Jacob was also known as Israel. His descendants came to be called the Israelites, or the Children of Israel.

This Canaanite vessel in the shape of a man's head was found at Jericho and dates to the 18th–19th centuries B.C.

Exodus from Egypt

Around 1700 B.C., the Israelites moved to Egypt because of a famine in Canaan. They were originally welcomed but later the Egyptians grew less tolerant of the Israelites and made them into slaves. Around 1250 B.C., the patriarch Moses led his people out of Egypt into the Sinai Desert. The book of Exodus in the Bible tells how Moses received a code of law called the Ten Commandments from God on the summit of Mount Sinai. The Commandments were inscribed on two stone tablets.

PATH OF THE ANCIENT HEBREWS

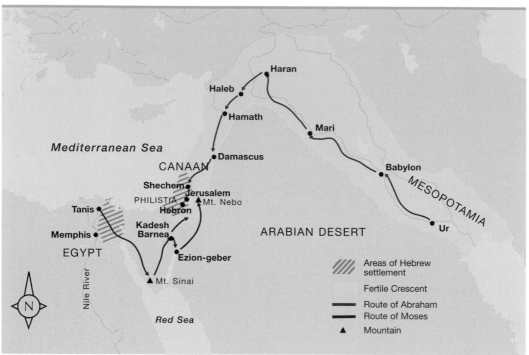

Haran

Haleb

Hamath

Mari

Mediterranean Sea

CANAAN   Damascus

Babylon

MESOPOTAMIA

Shechem
Jerusalem
PHILISTIA   ▲Mt. Nebo
Tanis   Hebron

Memphis

EGYPT

Kadesh
Barnea

Ezion-geber

ARABIAN DESERT

Ur

N

Nile River

▲ Mt. Sinai

Red Sea

/// Areas of Hebrew settlement

Fertile Crescent

Route of Abraham

Route of Moses

▲ Mountain

Ancient ancestors of the Hebrews followed the strip of land known as the Fertile Crescent out of Mesopotamia and into Canaan. Later, they settled in Egypt, but from here they were expelled into the desert and were led back to Canaan by Moses.

After 40 years in the desert, the Hebrews returned to Canaan. There they set out to win the land they believed God had promised them. Led by the hero Joshua, they laid siege to the Canaanite cities. According to the Bible, at the battle of Jericho, the troops of Joshua blew their horns, "and the walls came tumbling down."

The Hebrews conquered the Judaean Hills and the Jordan Valley. There they settled down and farmed. For the next 200 years, their main enemies were the Philistines, a highly developed people who lived on the Mediterranean coast near modern Gaza.

David and Solomon

Around 1050 B.C., the Hebrews were divided into 12 tribes. The leaders of the tribes, known as Judges, led their people into battle. Now the Hebrews decided that they wanted one king to rule them all. They elected Saul, a brave and clever general. Saul's successor was King David. According to the Bible, David began life as a shepherd and is famous for having killed in his youth a huge Philistine warrior named Goliath by supposedly firing a slingshot at him.

David defeated the Philistines and won a great kingdom that stretched from the Mediterranean coast north into Syria and south to the Red Sea. He conquered the city of Jerusalem and made it capital of the Israelite kingdom around 1000 B.C. The king placed a chest called the Ark of the Covenant, which contained the Ten Commandments, in a shrine in the city. Thus he made Jerusalem the spiritual home of the Jewish religion. Today all synagogues have a case representing the chest to contain scrolls of the Torah.

The Bible has proved the main source for the history of the kingdom of David. Little or no evidence has been found in the records of other nations.

David's son, Solomon, was another great king, famed for his wisdom. Solomon built a beautiful temple in Jerusalem where his people could worship God. After Solomon died, his kingdom was divided into two parts. The ten northern tribes established the kingdom of Israel in the north. The two southern tribes set up the kingdom of Judah in the south, which included Jerusalem (*see* p. 52). The word Jew comes from the name "Judah."

In the centuries that followed, the kingdoms came under the influence of other peoples in the region, including the great Assyrian empire and a highly civilized and skilled, seafaring people called the Phoenicians, who lived in the area to the north of Palestine, where modern Lebanon is today.

THE KINGDOM OF DAVID AND THE 12 TRIBES

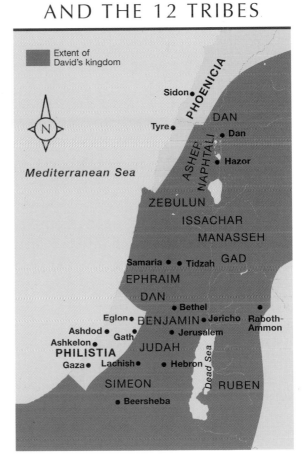

Extent of David's kingdom

PHOENICIA

Sidon

Tyre

Mediterranean Sea

DAN

Dan

ASHER

NAPHTALI

Hazor

ZEBULUN

ISSACHAR

MANASSEH

Samaria • • Tidzah   GAD

EPHRAIM

DAN

Bethel

Eglon • BENJAMIN • Jericho   Raboth-Ammon

Ashdod • Gath

Ashkelon •

PHILISTIA   JUDAH

Gaza • Lachish •   • Hebron

SIMEON

• Beersheba

Jerusalem

Dead Sea

RUBEN

THE KINGDOMS OF JUDAH AND ISRAEL

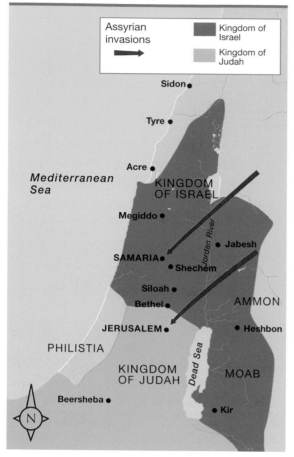

The map shows the kingdom of Israel, destroyed by Sargon II in 722 B.C., and the kingdom of Judah, destroyed by King Nebuchadnezzar in 586 B.C.

Foreign Rule

In 722 B.C., the northern kingdom of Israel was conquered by the Assyrians from the northeast. The ten northern tribes were exiled to distant lands and disappeared from history. They are known as the "ten lost tribes." A century later the Assyrians were defeated by the Babylonians, another powerful empire from what is now Iraq.

In 586 B.C., the Babylonians conquered Judah. They sacked the city of Jerusalem and destroyed Solomon's temple. The people were led in chains to Babylon and forced into slavery. The famous Psalm 137 in the Bible records their lament: "By the rivers of Babylon we sat down and wept when we remembered Zion." Zion was an ancient name for Jerusalem. The exile in Babylon lasted less than 50 years. In 539 B.C., another great empire, the Persians, defeated the Babylonians. The Persians allowed the Jews to return to their homeland and rebuilt the Jews' temple in Jerusalem.

The Persians ruled much of the Middle East for the next 200 years. Then, in 334 B.C., an ambitious young king, Alexander the Great, set out to conquer the world from Macedonia, to the north of Greece. Alexander defeated the Persians and took over their empire. When Alexander died, his empire was split into three parts. A general called Seleucus succeeded him in Palestine, the first of a line of rulers called the Seleucids who ruled the region until 200 B.C.

Under the Seleucids, the Greek way of life took hold in the land of Israel. Some Jews began worshiping Greek gods; others remained true to the Jewish religion. In 167 B.C., a new ruler, Antiochus IV, outlawed Judaism and ordered the people to worship Greek gods. He built an altar to the Greek gods in the temple in Jerusalem. The Jewish people rebelled, led by a family called the Maccabees, or Hasmoneans. The Jews were victorious and re-established the kingdom of Judah. They cleansed and rededicated the temple, an event commemorated by the Jewish festival of Hanukkah.

Hasmonean rule lasted for a century, but by 70 B.C. the kingdom was torn by civil war. The chaos allowed Roman troops to march into Judah in 63 B.C. For the next 500 years, Judah was a Roman province called Judea, part of the Roman empire. The province was ruled by a governor appointed by Rome.

The Maccabees' revolt against Greek rule (shown below) was a point of pride in Jewish history, provoking the two later unsuccessful revolts against the Romans.

Roman Rule

The most famous governor of Judaea was Herod, who was called "the Great." Herod ruled Judaea from 37 B.C. While a friend and ally of Rome, he was a convert to Judaism and given the title "King of the Jews," but the Jewish people resented him. He died around A.D. 4.

On Herod's death, his kingdom was divided among his three remaining sons. Jerusalem now came under the direct control of Rome, rather than a local administrator.

King Herod the Great

The Bible condemns King Herod as a brutal tyrant. The son of a Jewish nobleman and an Arabian princess, and himself a convert to Judaism, he is known to have murdered his wife and three of his own sons because he believed that they were plotting to overthrow him. According to Christian tradition, Herod also ordered the murder of all boys under the age of two in the town of Bethlehem. He had heard a prophecy that a leader born in Bethlehem would rise up to free the Jewish people.

Herod's rule was harsh, but during his reign (37– 4 B.C.), the Jews at least enjoyed a time of peace during which the Romans did not harass them. Herod was also a great builder. In addition to many fortresses, he built whole new towns such as the port of Caesarea, Palestinae, and Sebaste, several palaces in Jerusalem, and advanced drainage systems and aqueducts, such as that at Caesarea shown below. He rebuilt the temple in Jerusalem, making it so lavish it was considered one of the wonders of the world.

A time of turmoil began for Judaea. A number of different groups developed among the Jewish people. Each had its own vision of the future of the nation, but all hoped that God would send a savior or Messiah to expel the Romans and free the Jews.

It was in these troubled times that Jesus of Nazareth was born, around the year 4 B.C. When Jesus grew up, he began to teach in the Galilee region, then went to Jerusalem. Many people thought he was a wise teacher. Some believed he was the Messiah and the Son of God. The Romans may have seen him as a rebel leader who would stir up trouble and threaten their rule. We know that they arrested him, charged him with treason, and crucified him, in about A.D. 29.

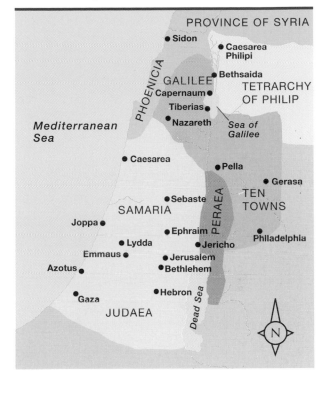

THE ROMAN PROVINCES OF PALESTINE

The map shows the Roman provinces of Palestine around the time of Jesus Christ's birth in about 4 B.C.

The First Jewish Revolt

At the time of Christ, the Jewish population in the ancient world was around eight million. In the following years, Rome appointed several harsh governors to rule Judaea, and the Jews suffered great hardship. In A.D. 66, they rebelled. Five years of fierce fighting followed. The Romans destroyed all Jewish towns that rose against them. The city of Jerusalem fell after a terrible siege, and Herod's temple was destroyed. In A.D. 73, the last rebel stronghold, the fortress of Masada was recaptured (*see* p. 23). The Romans sent 100,000 soldiers into Judaea to enforce their rule.

Jesus of Nazareth

Most of what we know of Jesus of Nazareth comes from the four gospels (books) of Matthew, Mark, Luke, and John. These texts make up much of the New Testament of the Christian Bible. According to the Christian tradition, the books were written by some of Christ's closest followers, or disciples, but many scholars now doubt that they were written by people who knew Jesus personally. According to the gospels, Jesus was born in Bethlehem in Judaea and spent his childhood in Nazareth. Around the age of 30, he began his public life, preaching near the Sea of Galilee. Much of Jesus' message was new and revolutionary. He stressed the importance of loving God and one's neighbors, and the doctrine of "turning the other cheek." He taught that the meek and poor would be rewarded in heaven. The gospels also state that Jesus healed the sick and performed many other amazing feats, or miracles.

Around the year A.D. 29, Jesus was arrested and charged with treason against Rome. The penalty was death by crucifixion—being nailed to a wooden cross. The Roman governor Pontius Pilate sentenced him to death. According to Christian tradition, he was crucified on a hill outside Jerusalem. His dead body was then sealed in a stone tomb.

Three days later, Mary Magdalen, one of Jesus' friends, found the tomb empty. The gospels then tell how Jesus appeared to his disciples several times in the next few days. Jesus' followers became convinced that God had raised Jesus from the dead. The gospels relate how, after 40 days, Jesus rose to heaven.

PERSECUTION AND THE DIASPORA

In the years that followed the First Jewish Revolt, life for the Jews became worse than ever. In A.D. 117, the Roman emperor Hadrian forbade the Jews to study their Bible and outlawed the Jewish custom of circumcision. It was not long before the Jews rebelled again, in A.D. 132. This time the rebels were led by a man called Simon Bar-Kochba, whose name means "Son of the Star." Again, the Romans cracked down ruthlessly, destroying more than 1,000 Jewish towns and villages.

In 135, Jerusalem was captured, destroyed, and rebuilt as a Roman city named Aelia Capitolina. The Jews were driven out of the city and forbidden to re-enter except on one day each year, which marked the anniversary of the temple's destruction. The province of Judaea was renamed Palestine, after the ancient Philistines.

Many Jews were executed or sold as slaves. Although some Jews became Christians, many more kept the Jewish religion. Others were exiled to foreign lands. Thousands fled from persecution, either immediately or in the following decades. Anti-Jewish hatred, which took several forms, lasted over many centuries. The Jews were despised not just for following a different religion, but because before their revolts they had been allowed special privileges to worship their God, and these were resented. The Jews scattered to establish more than 70 Jewish communities around the world. This event is called the Diaspora, or "dispersion." In their settlements, they kept Jewish beliefs and customs alive. Many of these dispersed Jewish communities still exist in some form.

The map shows the extent of the Diaspora and major centers of Jewish settlement up to around A.D. 500.

DIASPORA

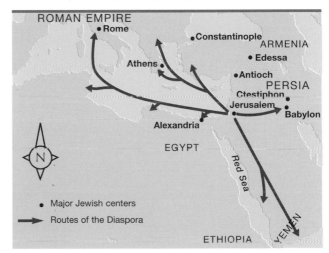

- Major Jewish centers
→ Routes of the Diaspora

The Rise of Christianity

Meanwhile the new religion of Christianity, based on Christ's teachings, took root first around the eastern Mediterranean and then throughout the Roman empire. For the first 300 years, the Romans persecuted and killed Christians for their faith. Not until A.D. 313 did the Roman emperor Constantine grant Christians the freedom to practice their religion. Soon, Christianity became the state religion of the Roman empire. Tens of thousands of people converted to Christianity, and the land where Jesus had lived became known as the Holy Land.

In A.D. 326 Constantine's mother, the Empress Helena, made a pilgrimage (religious journey) to the Holy Land. She visited Bethlehem, Nazareth, and Jerusalem and built churches to mark the places where it was thought Christ had lived and died. Christian pilgrims flocked to pay homage at the new churches. The Christian population of Palestine grew rapidly.

The map shows the extent of the Roman empire in A.D. 212, at its greatest extent.

THE ROMAN EMPIRE

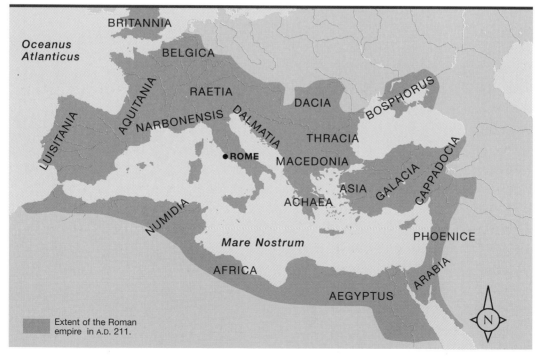

Oceanus Atlanticus

BRITANNIA

BELGICA

LUISITANIA

AQUITANIA

NARBONENSIS

RAETIA

DALMATIA

DACIA

THRACIA

BOSPHORUS

●ROME

MACEDONIA

ASIA

GALACIA

CAPPADOCIA

ACHAEA

NUMIDIA

Mare Nostrum

PHOENICE

AFRICA

ARABIA

AEGYPTUS

Extent of the Roman empire in A.D. 211.

N

The Roman emperor Constantine with his mother Helena. Together they were responsible for the early spread of Christianity in the Roman empire.

By A.D. 450 most people in Palestine were Christian, although there were still large Jewish communities, particularly in the north. The Jews were still subject to harsh laws and forbidden to enter Jerusalem.

In A.D. 330 Constantine moved his capital from Rome to the city of Byzantium, which was then renamed Constantinople (modern Istanbul) in his honor. Around A.D. 395, the Roman empire was divided into two parts. Palestine became part of the Eastern or Byzantine empire for nearly 250 years.

The Churches of Helena

Empress Helena, mother of Constantine, built the now-famous Church of the Nativity in Bethlehem and the Church of the Holy Sepulchre in Jerusalem. Her church in Bethlehem was built over the cave where it was believed that Jesus was born. It was altered considerably in A.D. 530 by Emperor Justinian. In Jerusalem, Helena built a church on the site of Jesus's crucifixion on the hill of Golgotha. Tradition relates that she discovered the cross on which Jesus was crucified.

Muslims believe that Jewish and Christian teachings are true, but that the revelations of Mohammed supersede them.

The Rise of Islam

Around A.D. 570, the prophet Mohammed was born in Mecca in Arabia. He founded a new religion called Islam, which was to become a great force in the world. During the early 600s, Mohammed had a series of visions that were later written down in the Islamic holy book, the Koran. The word Islam means "submission." Mohammed preached submission to the will of the one God, called Allah.

Mohammed believed that Arabs were also descended from Abraham, the father of the Hebrews. He taught that Islam should replace the Jewish and Christian religions. The prophet died in 632. On his death, his followers, called Muslims, carried on his vision.

The map shows the Islamic empire in about A.D. 800. The provinces of the empire shown here were ruled from Baghdad.

Fired by their new religion, Arab armies swept through the Middle East. Eventually, their empire stretched from Spain and northern Africa to India. In 640, they conquered Palestine. The region would

THE ISLAMIC WORLD

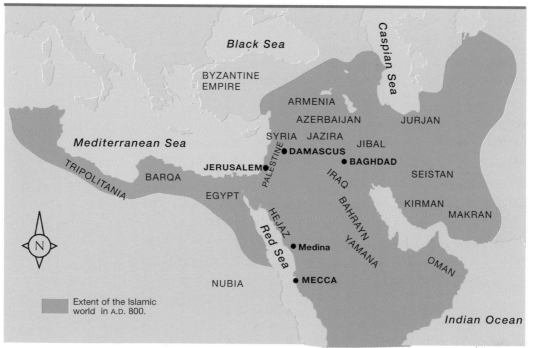

Extent of the Islamic world in A.D. 800.

remain in Muslim hands for much of the next 1,300 years, but there would be a number of different dynasties (ruling families).

Palestine's first Muslim rulers were the caliphs of the Omayyad dynasty. Their capital was Damascus in Syria. The caliphs toured the Holy Land, and each spot where they prayed became sacred to their own religion. The caliphs declared that the temple rock in Jerusalem, which Jews believed marked the spot where Abraham had offered to sacrifice his son Isaac, was also the place where Mohammed had ascended to heaven. They built a beautiful shrine, the Dome of the Rock, at the site around the year 700.

The interior of the ornate Islamic building, the Dome of the Rock, in East Jerusalem.

Muslims believed that the religious leaders of the Bible, including Abraham and Jesus, were prophets sent by God. Mohammed was God's greatest prophet. Jews and Christians were known as "the Peoples of the Book." They were granted the freedom to practice their religion, but it was hoped that they would convert to Islam. Gradually, most people in Palestine did absorb the culture of their rulers and became Muslims.

In 750, a second Muslim dynasty, the Abbasids, took over. They ruled from faraway Baghdad in what is now Iraq. In time, they were replaced by a third ruling family, the Fatimids, who ruled from Egypt. The Fatimids were harsh rulers who destroyed many Christian churches. In 1055, the Fatimids were overthrown by another Muslim dynasty, the Seljuks, who were Turks.

Holy Wars

By now Christianity had spread throughout Europe. During the 1000s, Christians had become increasingly concerned that the Holy Land where Jesus had lived lay in the hands of Muslims. Now the Seljuks started to attack Christian pilgrims. The Pope called upon Christian nations to join together to recapture Palestine. In 1096 thousands of Christians, nobles and commoners alike, set out on a military pilgrimage called a Crusade. Over the next three years, the Crusaders conquered much of the Holy Land. In 1099, they captured Jerusalem and killed most of its inhabitants, both Muslims and Jews.

The Christians set up several Latin states (*see* opposite) in Palestine, which lasted in various forms for about 200 years. This was a time of frequent fighting and hardship for the people of Palestine. In 1187 the Christian armies were defeated by Saladin, a mighty Muslim warrior who ruled Egypt and Syria. The battle took place at

The Crusader castle at Belvoir in northern Galilee was built by the French Knights Hospitalers in 1168. It fell to the Muslim forces in 1191 after three and a half years of siege.

the Horns of Hittim near Galilee. More waves of Crusaders arrived, led by King Louis VII of France and King Richard I of England. The Crusaders managed to recapture much of Palestine, but not Jerusalem. They ruled the land from a new capital, the port of Acre (modern Akko) on the Mediterranean.

Fighting continued on and off for the next century. In 1291 the Muslims finally ousted the Crusaders from Palestine. They destroyed Acre and the other Crusader ports and flooded parts of the coastal plain so the Christians could not return.

Palestine's new Muslim conquerors were the Mamluks, who ruled from Egypt. The Mamluks were freed slaves who had become an elite warrior group. They ruled the region for the next two centuries, but did not establish a strong government. They built many mosques, some of which still survive.

THE LATIN STATES, 1187

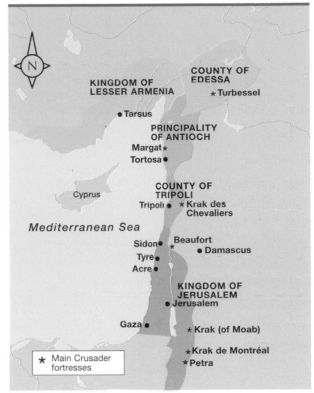

The map shows the Latin states in the Middle East in 1187 established by the Crusaders in the name of the Christian church.

Four Centuries of Turkish Rule

In 1517 the Ottoman Turks, who were also Muslims, defeated the Mamluks. Palestine became part of the enormous Ottoman empire, whose capital was Constantinople, which was renamed Istanbul. Turkish rule was to last for the next four centuries, until the end of World War I (1914–1918). The first Turkish sultans (rulers) were great builders. The sultan Suleyman the Magnificent (1520–1566) rebuilt parts of Jerusalem. The city walls he built still stand today.

THE OTTOMAN EMPIRE

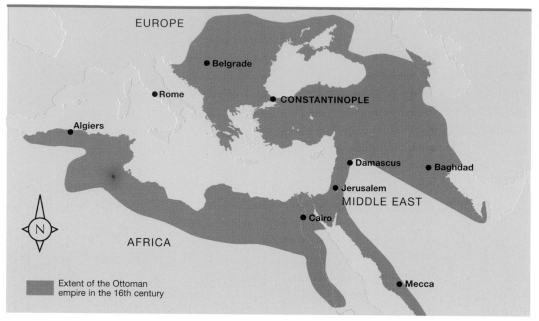

During the 15th and 16th centuries the Ottoman empire threatened to overrun Europe, but by the 19th century it had been weakened by corruption.

At first, Palestine prospered under Turkish rule. On the whole the Turks were tolerant and conditions were better than they had been under Christian rule. Despite some local mismanagement, the period was one of general prosperity and Jews began to occupy prominent positions in the administration and to contribute to Ottoman trade and industry. However, starting in the 17th century, the region was neglected as the Ottoman empire grew weaker. Powerful clans fought among each other to gain control over parts of Palestine as Turkish authority broke down. In the 19th century, foreign nations including Britain, France, and Russia began to take an interest in Palestine and covet control in the region. The British opened a consulate in Jerusalem in 1838, promising to protect the rights of Jews and Druze in Syria and Palestine and the religious sites that were holy to both Christianity and Judaism. However, the British government was probably more motivated by securing its international trade interests in the region than by any concern for religious sites.

THE RETURN TO PALESTINE

Meanwhile, Jews had started to return to Palestine. Since the beginning of the Diaspora, Jews had settled in many parts of Europe. From the earliest centers in Egypt, Rome, and Babylonia (now Iraq), Jewish communities had sprung up around the Mediterranean. Spain had become a center of Jewish learning. From southern Europe, Jews spread north to settle in Germany, France, England, Russia, and Eastern Europe, particularly Poland.

Anti-Semitism

Throughout the medieval period, Jews suffered hardship and persecution. In European cities they were forced to live in separate districts called ghettos. In the 1340s, Jews were blamed for the spread of the bubonic plague, known as the Black Death. Anti-Semitism (hatred of Jews) became so extreme that whole communities of Jews were slaughtered in organized massacres called pogroms. During the 1490s, all Jews living in Spain and Portugal were expelled unless they converted to Christianity. Some made their way back to Palestine.

The Ghetto Nuovo or New Ghetto in Venice took its name from the Venetian for foundry (getto). During the medieval period, Jews were forced to live in such separate areas in many European cities.

Anti-Jewish feeling grew in eastern and western Europe. In the 1640s, tens of thousands of Jews were massacred during a time of war in Poland. In the 1880s, massacres took place in Russia and Eastern Europe. Each wave of persecution drove Jews to more distant lands. Many emigrated to North and South America, particularly to the United States, where, for the first time, they were allowed to become full citizens of a country. Others returned to Palestine.

Zionism was much stronger in Eastern Europe than it was in the west. This was because there was greater anti-Semitism in the east, compared with the relative tolerance of countries such as Germany and France.

Zionism

The late 1800s saw the birth of a new Jewish movement called Zionism. Zion was an old biblical name for Jerusalem. Zionists called for a Jewish state to be re-established in Palestine, as a solution to anti-Semitism. Two of the early leaders were Theodor Herzl (1860–1904, *see* box opposite), whose influential pamphlet *The Jewish State* was published in 1896, and a shrewd diplomat named Chaim Weizmann (1874–1952).

In 1897, the Zionists held their first world conference. Between 1880 and 1903, tens of thousands of Jews moved to Palestine in the first wave of organized immigration, which was called an *aliyah*. More *aliyahs* followed. In Palestine, the Zionists bought land and set up farming communities. Later they founded a new city, Tel Aviv. Trouble flared between the new settlers and the Arab inhabitants of Palestine, but still the immigrants flooded in. By 1914, 700,000 people lived in Palestine. Of these, 615,000 were Arabs and 85,000 were Jews. Meanwhile, European countries such as Britain grew even more eager to influence events in the Middle East.

"A Jewish National Home"

In 1914 World War I began. Turkey supported Germany against the Allies, who included Britain, France, Russia, and later the United States. The Allies planned to divide the Ottoman empire among them if they won the war. During the war, Palestinian Jews and Arabs supported British troops fighting Turkish troops in Palestine. Urged on by Chaim Weizmann, the British government announced it would support the establishment of a "Jewish national home" in Palestine. This statement was known as the Balfour Declaration (*see* box p. 68), after the British foreign minister, Lord Balfour. At the same time, however, Britain also promised Arabs support for an Arab state in the same region.

World War I ended in 1918 with defeat for Germany and Turkey. The League of Nations, an international

Theodor Herzl

Theodor Herzl was the founder of political Zionism, the movement that was formed at the end of the 19th century to establish a Jewish homeland. Herzl was born in 1860 in Budapest, Hungary. After studying law in Vienna, Austria, he became a journalist and writer. During a term working in Paris, France, for an Austrian newspaper, Herzl witnessed the vicious anti-Semitism that re-emerged in France in 1894 following the court-martial (military trial) and wrongful conviction of a Jewish army officer named Alfred Dreyfus.

Until then, Herzl had believed in integration for the Jews, who had been living in ghettos for centuries in countries such as Poland. Like many European thinkers of the time, Herzl thought that Jews mixing with others in the Christian societies of Europe would bring an end to anti-Semitism. Jews would be recognized as true nationals and often patriots of the countries they lived in and their separate status would end without them having to give up their religion. However, the reaction of people in France to the Dreyfus trial affected him so much that he changed his mind completely. He now felt that the Jews had to become a separate national group in their own right and that this would be the only guarantee of their future safety and fulfillment.

In 1896 Herzl published a pamphlet, *Der Judenstaat* (*The Jewish State*). He was the first to press for recognition of Zionism by other countries. At the first Zionist congress, which Herzl called in Basel, Switzerland, in 1897, Palestine was chosen as the location of the future Jewish state. It was regarded by many Jews of the Diaspora as the natural Jewish homeland to which all Jews could return. The World Zionist Organization was also established to help provide economic support for the proposed state.

Because Palestine was then part of Turkey, Herzl tried to set up negotiations with the Turkish ruler, Sultan Abdulhamid II, and other political leaders and financiers, but no-one was prepared to offer any support. Herzl died in 1904. His goal of achieving a Jewish homeland would only be fulfilled 44 years later.

The Balfour Declaration

This statement was issued by the British government on November 9, 1917, thus ensuring the support of Zionists for the British cause in the war effort. The central passage read as follows:

"His Majesty's Government view with favour the establishment of a national home for the Jewish people and will use their best endeavours to facilitate the achievement of this object, it being clearly understood that nothing shall be done which may prejudice the civil and religious rights of existing non-Jewish communities in Palestine, or the rights and political status enjoyed in any other country."

organization formed to promote world peace, commissioned Britain to administer Palestine on a temporary basis. Under the terms of the commission, Britain was to help the Jews establish their own national home there. Palestinian Arabs opposed this plan.

The 1920s saw increasing conflict between Arabs and Jews, as tens of thousands of Jews emigrated to Palestine. In the 1930s, thousands more arrived, fleeing persecution in Nazi Germany and Poland. In Germany, the Nazis, led by Adolf Hitler, began their campaign of terror against Jews on an everyday basis. Laws were passed enabling the seizure of Jewish property and excluding Jews from every walk of life (*see* opposite). By 1936, Palestinian Arabs had become so alarmed by mass Jewish immigrations that they rebelled against British rule. In 1939 the British government responded by clamping down on Jewish immigration and the sale of land to Jews.

The Holocaust

In 1939 World War II began. Germany, Italy, and Japan, known as the Axis powers, fought the Allies, who included Britain, France, and later the United States and the Soviet Union. In the early years of the war, the Germans conquered much of Europe, but later, the tide of war turned against them. They surrendered in 1945. During the war, the Nazis murdered six million Jews—two-thirds of all the Jews in Europe. The Jews were gassed, shot, or starved in concentration camps. This terrible mass murder is called the Holocaust.

The Holocaust

The word Holocaust refers to perhaps the most horrific event of the 20th century: the planned mass extermination of over six million Jews and millions of other peoples by the German Nazi regime during the period 1941–1945. This policy was a result of the racist views of the Nazi leader Adolf Hitler and his supporters.

Hitler's Nazis came to power in Germany in 1933 and gradually began excluding Jews from public life and business there. This culminated in the Nuremberg Laws of 1935, which deprived Jews of citizenship. There were also pogroms (massacres) of Jews in Germany and Czechoslovakia, which the Nazis had occupied in 1938. After 1941 the Nazis formulated the "Final Solution." In the countries under Nazi control Jews were rounded up and transported in cattle cars to concentration camps. Once there, they were either worked or starved to death or immediately shot or gassed in specially built extermination chambers.

The effect of the Holocaust has been incalculable. Whole Jewish communities in Eastern Europe were wiped out; one-third of all Jews in the world were killed. Nazi persecution led to mass immigration to Israel before, during, and after the war, and created a passionate argument for the creation of a Jewish homeland.

This memorial at the Holocaust Museum in Jerusalem commemorates the 1.5 million Jewish children who died in the Holocaust.

TOWARD INDEPENDENCE

With the end of the war, conflict reawakened between Jews, Arabs, and the British in Palestine. After the experience of the Holocaust, the Jews were even more determined to have a homeland where they would be safe. The old League of Nations had been replaced by a new organization called the United Nations. In 1947, the United Nations voted to divide Palestine into two separate states for Jews and Arabs. The Jews accepted the plan they drew up. The Arabs rejected it.

Irgun Zvai Leumi

Irgun Zvai Leumi ("National Military Organization") was a Jewish right-wing terrorist organization that was founded in 1931. Irgun's members aimed to establish a Jewish state on both sides of the Jordan River and advocated the use of violence to achieve their aims. They organized terrorist activities and carried out assassinations of British nationals whom they regarded as illegal occupiers of Palestine. They also helped enable many illegal immigrants to enter the country after the British tightened Palestine's immigration laws in the 1930s.

Irgun's members were very disciplined and could be extremely violent. In 1947, they raided an Arab village, Dayr Yasin, and killed all 254 inhabitants.

The Birth of the State

On May 14, 1948, Britain withdrew from Palestine. The Jews declared the birth of an independent Jewish state called Israel. The next day, five Arab nations launched attacks on the new country. The conflict developed into the War of Independence, which lasted until 1949. During the war, Israel succeeded in defending its borders. In addition, it overran about half of the land the United Nations had proposed as an Arab state. The Palestinian Arabs called this *al-Naqba* ("the catastrophe"), for they now had no homeland of their own.

In 1949 Israel was accepted as a member of the United Nations. Chaim Weizmann was the country's first president; David Ben-Gurion (1886–1973) was the first prime minister. During the 1950s, large numbers of Jews continued to arrive to help build the new country. Industry and farming were developed, and new towns were built.

A Nation at War

Meanwhile, conflict between Israel and its neighbors continued. In 1956, supported by Britain and France, Israel attacked Egypt for its seizure of the Suez Canal. Israel occupied Egypt's huge Sinai Peninsula and the Gaza Strip, but withdrew its troops after the war ended.

In 1966 and 1967, sporadic fighting broke out again, this time between Israel and Egypt, Jordan, and Syria. In the space of only six days in June 1967, Israel defeated its enemies. It reoccupied Sinai and the Gaza

The Suez Crisis

The Suez Crisis was caused by the Egyptian government's seizure of the Suez Canal and its revenues in order to fund the building of a dam in southern Egypt. The Suez Canal Company was partly owned by the French and British governments and both attacked Egypt, occupying the canal zone. Attacks were also launched by Israel, escalating hostilities sparked by repeated Egyptian raids on Israeli territory. U.S. and Soviet opposition to the French and British action led to their withdrawal in December 1956. Israel also withdrew but secured shipping rights in the area. The real victors were President Nasser of Egypt and the cause of Egyptian nationalism.

ISRAEL IN 1967

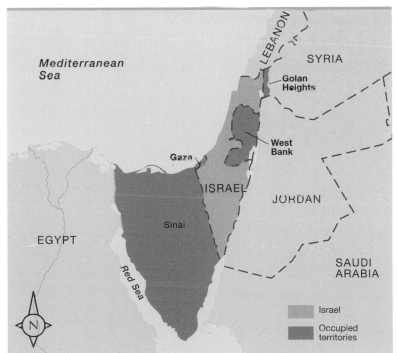

The map shows the Middle East after the Six-Day War which began on June 5, 1967.

The Palestine Liberation Organization (PLO)

Founded in 1964, the PLO became active after the 1967 war, aiming to establish an Arab state in Palestine. From 1969 it was led by Yasser Arafat (born 1929, below). It included guerrilla groups which from the late 1960s launched a series of attacks against civilian and military targets in Israel. In response, Israel raided PLO bases in neighboring Arab countries. In 1974 the PLO renounced violence outside Israel and sought a Palestinian state in Gaza and the West Bank.

Strip. It also captured the Golan Heights from Syria and the West Bank and East Jerusalem, from Jordan. The occupied areas were home to about one million Palestinian Arabs. East Jerusalem and the Golan Heights were taken under Israeli control.

The Yom Kippur War

In 1973, full-scale war broke out again. Egypt and Syria launched an attack on Israel on Yom Kippur, the Jews' holiest day. During the Yom Kippur War, Israel held on to the territory it had occupied in 1967, but suffered heavy losses and was brought very close to total defeat. The fighting died down in 1974.

Saudi Arabia and Kuwait provided funds for the Arab forces in the Yom Kippur War, making it possible for Egypt and Syria to acquire Soviet weapons. The oil-rich Arab countries began to use their economic muscle effectively, halting all oil exports to the United States and other Western nations as a crippling response for their aid to Israel. This embargo (ban) on oil to the West caused huge economic problems and led to gasoline rationing in many Western countries. Eventually, massive economic and military funding from the United States was needed to help Israel recover from the Yom Kippur War, but this could not stop Israel's economy from going into crisis for several years, with prices rising steeply.

In 1978, the Egyptian president Anwar al-Sadat (1918–1981) and the Israeli prime minister Menachem Begin (1913–1992) met with U.S. president Jimmy Carter at Camp David in the United States. A formal peace agreement followed in 1979. Israel withdrew from Sinai over the next four years. President Sadat was the first Arab leader to recognize Israel.

Golda Meir (1898–1978)

Golda Meir was prime minister of Israel from 1969 to 1974. She was also a founder of the State of Israel. Meir was born Goldie Mabovitz on May 3, 1898, in Kiev in Ukraine. She emigrated to Milwaukee, Wisconsin, with her family in 1906 and became a Zionist while a teenager. In 1921, she emigrated from the United States to Palestine.

Meir was involved in both the Zionist and labor movements in the 1930s and 1940s in Palestine and also sought support for Zionism in Europe and the United States. In 1948, she signed the independence proclamation and served as minister of labor and social insurance in Israel's first Knesset. From 1956 to 1966 she was minister of foreign affairs, changing her name to its Hebrew version, Golda Meir. Three years later, she became Israel's first woman prime minister. Her premiership was marked by her seach for a peace settlement in the Middle East and she traveled widely, visiting the Vatican and Romania, and playing host to Chancellor Brandt of Germany. She resigned her post in 1974 mainly as a result of Israel's lack of readiness in the Yom Kippur War (*see* opposite). Meir died in Jerusalem on December 8, 1978.

Palestinians demonstrate with the outlawed Palestinian flag in the West Bank town of Bet Sachour in 1988.

The Intifada

The 1970s and 1980s saw growing conflict between Israel and the PLO. Among many incidents, one in particular drew world attention: in 1972, PLO terrorists captured and killed 11 Israeli athletes during the Olympic Games in Munich, Germany. After 1974, however, the PLO renounced terrorists attacks on targets outside Israel and sought to work for a Palestinian state in the West Bank. In 1982, Israel attacked southern Lebanon, from where the PLO had launched attacks on Israel. Fighting continued in Lebanon for three years, after which Israeli troops withdrew except from the border zone.

In 1987, Arabs in the West Bank and Gaza Strip began a campaign of violent demonstrations against the continuing Israeli occupation. This was known as the *intifada* (Arabic for "uprising"). During the early 1990s, the United States, Israel's main ally, pressed Israel to take steps to resolve its conflict with the PLO. In 1994, Israel signed a peace treaty with Jordan.

The Persian Gulf War

Conflict in the Persian Gulf broke out in January and February 1991 following the invasion of Kuwait by Iraq. The United States and its coalition partners, including European and Arab countries, attacked Iraq. Israel backed the anti-Iraq coalition but was not involved in combat. However, this did not prevent the Iraqi dictator Saddam Hussein (born 1937) from ordering Scud missiles to be fired at Israeli territory.

These Iraqi attacks caused injuries to 200 people and damaged 9,000 homes in Tel Aviv. Unusually for Israel, it did not hit back, largely because of the delicacy of the situation and due to pressure from the United States. There was a risk that if Israel entered the war, then Arab states would leave the anti-Iraq coalition.

In 1993, PLO leader Yasser Arafat and Israeli prime minister Yitzhak Rabin (1922–1995) signed an historic peace agreement that committed Israel to plan its withdrawal from the West Bank and Gaza Strip, and for Arab areas within these regions to be given self-rule. Between 1995 and 1997, all Arab areas in the West Bank were transferred to Palestinian rule.

Israeli prime minister Yitzhak Rabin and PLO leader Yasser Arafat shake hands on the White House lawn in September 1993 after the signing of the historic Oslo Accords.

The Assassination of Rabin

On November 4, 1995, Yitzhak Rabin was assassinated by a fanatical Jewish student opposed to the peace process and the handing over of land to the Palestinians. People throughout Israel and the world were deeply shocked at what was the first assassination of a Jewish leader by a Jew. However, the killing of Rabin brought to the surface the intense feelings dividing the Israeli people over the peace process. Many of the Jewish religious parties opposed any handover of land. They wanted to continue the building of settlements in the areas occupied by Israel in war and opposed any attempt of governments to halt that con-

Terrorism Against Israel

Arab terrorist groups include Hezbollah, which is active in Syria and Lebanon, and Hamas, the most extreme of the Palestinian organizations that reject the peace process. Both of these groups have waged bomb attacks on Israeli military and civilian targets. Many attacks have been on busloads of citizens in crowded areas or in the disputed border regions.

Retaliation by Israel has often been swift and brutal. In January 1996, Israeli troops assassinated a Palestinian, Yahya Ayyash, who was suspected of being the brains behind a number of suicide bomb attacks (where the bombers are killed along with their victims) against Israelis. Hamas retaliated with further suicide bombings in Jerusalem during February and March 1996, killing more than 60 people and wounding over 100. Israeli prime minister Shimon Peres responded by temporarily closing Israel's borders with the West Bank and Gaza Strip.

Terrorism has aroused a widespread feeling among many Israelis that peace comes at too high a price—and that such a fragile peace does not guarantee Israel's security. All of Israel's leaders have had to reassure the people that their security would be protected, while making gradual concessions to demands of its Arab neighbors, such as giving up territory won in war and making provisions for the homeless Palestinians. For example, to prove his commitment to Israel's security, Shimon Peres ordered Israeli troops to strike back at Hezbollah in southern Lebanon after repeated rocket attacks against northern Israel. This response led to weeks of fighting and the deaths of hundreds of Lebanese civilians. Mistrust of the peace process was reinforced by the prime minister who succeeded Shimon Peres, Benjamin Netanyahu, who speeded up the building of Jewish settlements on the West Bank and in East Jerusalem.

struction. Rabin's successor, Shimon Peres, had to contend with these and many other problems, and lost power in 1996 to his rival, Benjamin Netanyahu, leader of the Likud party.

Toward a Palestinian Homeland

In 1994, Palestinian authorities were given control over most of the Gaza Strip and the town of Jericho. In January 1996, the first general elections for the Palestinians of the West Bank, Gaza Strip, and East Jerusalem were held. Yasser Arafat won a resounding victory and was made responsible for government in the West Bank and Gaza Strip. Hopes for a lasting peace in the region looked brighter than they had for many years, but a number of difficult issues still remained to be resolved.

In 2000 in a dramatic echo of the negotiations between Israel and Egypt in 1979, the Israeli prime minister Ehud Barak and Palestinian leader Yasser Arafat met with U.S. president Bill Clinton at the U.S. presidential retreat at Camp David for further peace talks. The talks revolved around the question of East Jerusalem, which the Palestinians wanted to make the capital of a new Palestinian state. The Israelis however were unwilling to relinquish such an important site for the Jewish religious community and although plans for joint sovereignty of the city were discussed, no resolution was reached. Commentators now believe that the issue of Jerusalem is the main barrier to a lasting peace.

The Palestinian flag is almost identical to that of Jordan, where many Palestinians live. Jordan's flag has a white star on the red triangle. Jordan ceded its claim to the West Bank to the Palestinians in 1988.

Defense

Israel receives more American economic and military aid than any other nation. The country's armed forces are among the best equipped and most highly trained in the world. Total armed forces number 175,000. An additional 430,000 Israelis serve in the reserve forces. Men and women have to serve in the armed forces when they are 18 years old. Men serve for three years; women for 18 months. Military service is compulsory for Jews and Druze, but not for Israeli Muslims and Christians.

Israel has the largest defense industry originating within its own territory in the Middle East. The country has developed much of its own military aircraft and advanced weapons systems, including missiles such as the Jericho 2, which has a possible range of 930 miles (1,500 km).

Israel is believed to have a substantial arsenal of nuclear weapons—both atomic and hydrogen bombs—although the country has never confirmed this.

ISRAEL'S ADMINISTRATION

Israel is a democratic republic. The head of state is the president. This role is largely ceremonial, like that of the British king or queen. The president is elected for a five-year term and can serve only two consecutive (following) terms. The most powerful political figure is the prime minister, who is head of government, and is elected for a maximum of four years. Normally, he or she is leader of the party that holds the most seats in parliament. The prime minister heads the cabinet, the part of the government that decides what policies to pursue, which consists of ministers who are each responsible for a different area of policy (e.g. health, defense, education, etc.).

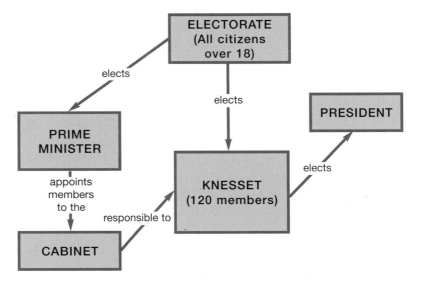

Israel is divided into six administrative regions: Jerusalem, Tel Aviv, and Haifa, and the northern, central, and southern districts (*see* p. 17). Each area is governed by a regional or town council.

There are both religious and lay (nonreligious) courts in Israel. The Supreme Court is the highest court. Jews, Muslims, Christians, and Druze all have their own religious courts, which hear cases relating to matters such as inheritance, marriage, and divorce.

Parliament and Elections

Israel's parliament, the Knesset, has only one "house," unlike the United States' Congress. There are 120 members, elected for a four-year term. Members of parliament do not represent a particular area, but are chosen from lists drawn up by each party. These lists rank candidates in order of importance and political parties are then given the number of seats that reflects their share of the vote, working down their list from the top.

Israel's voting system makes it difficult for one party to get a majority in parliament. Often, the government is a coalition (alliance) of different parties. In practice, this means that small parties have considerable power, as they may help to form the government. In recent years the religious parties have held the balance of power.

Political Parties

Israel has many political parties. The two main parties are the left-wing Labor Party, and the more conservative Likud Party. Although Israel has a strong secular tradition, the smaller religious parties have grown in political influence in recent years. Shas is a party of Orthodox Sephardic Jews—Jews originating from Spain or the Middle East—and has a large representation in the Knesset. The National Religious Party advocates strict adherence to the Jewish religion and tradition. Agudat Israel is another Orthodox Jewish party.

In addition to the main Labor and Likud parties, the Israeli parliament is composed of a large number of small parties representing different ethnic or religious groups. The larger parties are dependent on these groups to form a government.

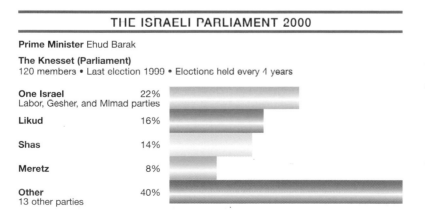

THE ISRAELI PARLIAMENT 2000

Prime Minister Ehud Barak

The Knesset (Parliament)
120 members • Last election 1999 • Elections held every 4 years

Party	Percentage
One Israel Labor, Gesher, and Mimad parties	22%
Likud	16%
Shas	14%
Meretz	8%
Other 13 other parties	40%

The Economy

"Our job is to harness the sun, sweeten the sea, and thus shall you make the desert bloom."

Israel's first prime minister David Ben-Gurion

In 1948, Israel was a poor country whose farming and industry had not been developed. Since then, particularly in the 1950s and 1960s, the economy has grown in leaps and bounds. Israelis are a skillful and hardworking people who put in long hours, six days a week. Despite few natural resources and high inflation (price rises), the country's industries are well developed, and Israelis enjoy high living standards.

Israel's economy depends greatly on defense and services. Israel's service industries provide around 81 percent of the country's gross national product (GNP)—the total value of goods and services produced in a year. Service industries include government services, health, education, transportation, tourism, and financial trade, which includes banking and insurance. Manufacturing and mining provide 17 percent of Israel's GNP. Farming makes up the remaining 2 percent.

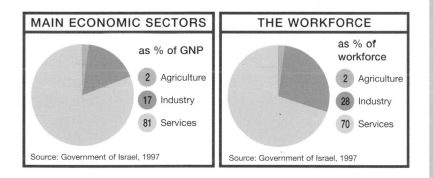

MAIN ECONOMIC SECTORS

as % of GNP

- 2 Agriculture
- 17 Industry
- 81 Services

Source: Government of Israel, 1997

THE WORKFORCE

as % of workforce

- 2 Agriculture
- 28 Industry
- 70 Services

Source: Government of Israel, 1997

The development of tourism, such as in the resort of Eilat on the Red Sea, has played an important part in boosting Israel's economy with foreign funds.

MAIN TRADING PARTNERS

EXPORTS

%

32.1	United States
6.2	United Kingdom
5.3	Hong Kong
5	Belgium/Luxembourg
3.3	Japan
48.1	Others

IMPORTS

%

19	United States
12	Belgium/Luxembourg
9	Germany
8	United Kingdom
7	Italy
45	Others

Source: Government of Israel, 1997

Israel's economy is dominated by its relations with the United States, although this is less so now than in the past.

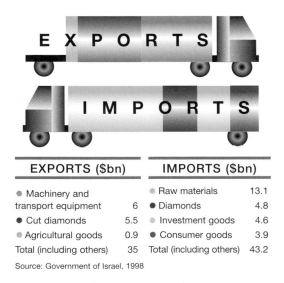

EXPORTS ($bn)		IMPORTS ($bn)	
● Machinery and transport equipment	6	● Raw materials	13.1
● Cut diamonds	5.5	● Diamonds	4.8
● Agricultural goods	0.9	● Investment goods	4.6
Total (including others)	35	● Consumer goods	3.9
		Total (including others)	43.2

Source: Government of Israel, 1998

About 50 percent of all businesses in Israel are privately owned. The state owns about 25 percent, and the remaining quarter are owned and run by the federation of trade unions, which is called Histadrut.

ISRAEL'S TRADE

With few natural resources, the total value of Israel's imports is always more than its exports, which causes problems with its trade balance. Inflation and high military spending have added to the country's economic difficulties. Israel's main trading partners are the United States and the countries of the European Union (EU), including Britain, Germany, Italy, and France. In the past, war has prevented trade with many of Israel's neighbors. Now the peace moves of recent years have brought new trade agreements with Jordan, Egypt, and North African nations. If a lasting peace is achieved, Israel, with its highly developed infrastructure, should dominate the economy in the region.

Israel's chief imports are mainly raw materials: chemicals, oil, coal, iron and steel, rough diamonds, grains, and also machinery, military equipment, and vehicles. The country's main asset is its skilled workforce, and its exports are mostly processed goods, such as chemical products, fertilizers, cut diamonds, electronic equipment, arms, foods, clothing, and also citrus fruit and other crops.

MAIN ECONOMIC SECTORS

Israel's economy has shifted its emphasis from agriculture to highly developed industry. Agriculture was initially important for Israel's survival because of the country's isolation in the Middle East. However, with the arrival of more highly skilled workers from abroad, it has made better economic sense for the country to import raw materials and concentrate on manufacturing.

FARMING

At the time of independence in 1948, Israel had little farmland, with mainly poor, rocky soil. Much of the land was desert or swamp, and most farm work was done by hand. In the last 50 years, the swamps have been drained and many parts of the deserts watered. Now one-fifth of Israel is fertile farmland, and much agricultural work is done by machines. Israel is now famous for its farm produce, including oranges and other tropical fruits, cotton, and cut flowers. The country is largely self sufficient in food, although it must still import some goods.

The main obstacle to farming in Israel is the lack of water. Most of the rainfall is in the north, and the main sources of freshwater, Lake Kinneret and the Jordan River, are also located there. The south receives very little rainfall but has fertile soil. In the 1960s, the National Water Carrier system was developed to solve this problem. This network of pumping stations, pipelines, and canals brings water all the way from the low-lying north to the fertile plateaus of the south.

HOW ISRAEL USES ITS LAND

- Cropland
- Forest
- Pasture
- Desert

Greening the Desert

In many dry parts of Israel, irrigation has been used to transform barren land into fertile fields. But the water is too precious just to be sprayed over the earth by

LAND USE

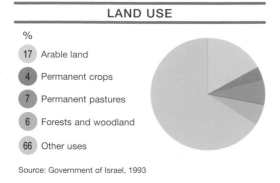

%

17 Arable land

4 Permanent crops

7 Permanent pastures

6 Forests and woodland

66 Other uses

Source: Government of Israel, 1993

Israel makes remarkably efficient use of its available land, although the percentage of usable land is still very low.

The healthy, outdoor life is a hallmark of Israeli culture, and workers on the kibbutzim, such as those here picking grapefruit, continue to work in the fields into their sixties and seventies.

sprinklers. Instead, Israeli scientists invented the system of drip irrigation, which is now widely used. Snaking across the fields, lines of thin plastic pipes with feeder holes deliver just the right amount of water and fertilizer to each plant's roots, drip by drip. The system is fine-tuned by computers. There are also desalination plants to remove salt from water, and underground wells. The technique of cloud-seeding—dispersing particles of silver iodide and other substances in clouds by aircraft to produce rainfall—was pioneered in Israel, although it is used sparingly.

Citrus fruits are one of Israel's main crops. Oranges, lemons, and tangerines are all produced in large quantities, both for export and the home market. Israel is among the world's top five grapefruit producers.

The Kibbutzim

In Israel, most farms are run as collective or cooperative communities, where members of the community work the fields together and share the profits. A kibbutz (plural: kibbutzim) is a collective farm. The community may contain anywhere from 100 to 1,000 members, known as kibbutzniks. Members eat together and share all decisions about the running of the kibbutz. In the past, kibbutz children between the ages of 13 and 18 often lived in separate houses, but now they mainly live

Even younger members of the kibbutz contribute to the work: here, children weed out quack grass.

with their parents. They are schooled by members of the kibbutz, whom they address by their first names.

A moshav (plural: moshavim) is another kind of cooperative farming community. Each family in the moshav has its own plot of land to farm, but the community provides equipment and supplies and sells the produce.

Israel's first kibbutz was established on the West Bank of the Jordan in 1909, and more appeared during Jewish immigration to Palestine in the early part of the 20th century. After independence in 1948, many kibbutzim were established along Israel's vulnerable frontiers. They were a vital element in defending the new nation, and many have been attacked at regular intervals by Palestinian forces.

In the 1980s and 1990s, many kibbutzniks left to look for jobs in the cities, and some kibbutzim have subsequently changed the way they use their land from farming to housing. However, the kibbutzim have often been hailed as a successful attempt at a communal way of life, and large numbers of young people from overseas still volunteer to live and work on them.

Hydroponics

Lack of water in Israel has led the country to become a leader in hydroponics, the growing of plants in nutrient solutions. In the Ein Gedi system, plants are grown with their roots immersed in a flowing solution. Other methods include growing in tuff (volcanic ash), which holds water and air very well, and sand culture, where water has to be constantly dribbled onto the plants. Cabutz, a mixture of water and manure, is also used. Here the liquid acts as fertilizer and solids as the growing medium.

One-third of Israel's citrus crop is sent abroad, either as whole fruit or processed juice. Other fruits, including melons, bananas, mangoes, avocados, strawberries, grapes, and dates, are also grown.

Vegetables that grow well in Israel include tomatoes, cucumbers, chickpeas, potatoes, and carrots. Grain crops include wheat, corn, and barley. Cotton is another important export crop, mainly harvested by machines. Israel is also famous for cut flowers, including long-stemmed roses, tulips, and carnations. Sunflowers are grown for their oil. Sheep, chickens, turkeys, and cattle are raised in many parts of Israel. Even pigs are raised to produce pork for export, despite the fact that religious Jews and Muslims do not eat pork. Fish are farmed in ponds and in cages in the sea at Eilat.

The lack of freshwater and natural streams in Israel has led the country to develop the farming of fish in large artificial ponds, such as those on the right, and in large cages off the Israeli coast.

ISRAEL'S INDUSTRY

Because of its lack of natural resources, Israel has concentrated its energies on manufacturing, importing raw materials from abroad and transforming them into manufactured goods. This has been made possible by the country's highly educated workforce, often supplemented by experts arriving from abroad—as in the recent influx of trained professionals from the former Soviet Union.

MAJOR INDUSTRIES

Israel's industry is concentrated around the cities along its Mediterranean coast, with other important centers at Jerusalem and the Arab city of Beersheba. The small size of the country makes transportation easy, and industry is relatively coordinated and well planned.

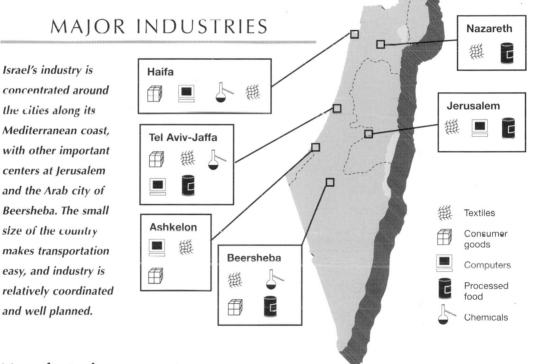

Nazareth

Haifa

Jerusalem

Tel Aviv-Jaffa

Ashkelon

Beersheba

Textiles

Consumer goods

Computers

Processed food

Chemicals

Manufacturing

During the early 20th century, there was very little industry in Palestine. Both before and after independence, immigrants included scientists and trained technicians, many of them refugees from Nazi Germany and occupied Europe, who brought new skills and expertise to the country. After 1948 Israel industrialized rapidly, helped by financial backing from many nations, especially the United States. Now manufacturing accounts for 17 percent of the country's gross national product and employs more than one-quarter of Israel's workers. Tel Aviv and Haifa are

The Working Week

Israelis are an industrious people who regularly work longer hours than employees in many other countries. The working week lasts six days. Only the Sabbath (*Shabat*)—Saturday—is a day of rest. Sunday is an ordinary working day. Recently, however, this practice has begun to change, as more Israelis take time off on Friday, when the Sabbath begins at sundown. Children also attend school six days a week. The working day starts at 7:00 or 8:00 A.M., and often lasts until 4:00 P.M. or late into the evening. Despite this, Israelis have a reputation for playing as well as working hard!

two of the main centers for industry. During the 1950s and 1960s, construction was a major industry; it boomed again in the 1990s with renewed economic prosperity.

Diamond-cutting is a key industry in Israel. No diamonds are actually mined in the country, but they are imported in their rough form and cut and polished into sparkling gems. The diamond industry dates back to the 1940s, when Jewish diamond-cutters from the Netherlands and Belgium fled Nazi persecution for Israel. Now Israel is the world's leader in diamond-cutting and polishing. It supplies a high proportion of the world's finished gems to make fine jewelry. Diamond is the hardest substance known, so it is also used to make industrial drilling and cutting tools.

Israel's unions

Histadrut, the General Federation of Labor, is Israel's famous organization of trade unions. Established in the 1920s, the federation is still powerful today, playing a key role in winning fair wages and good conditions for Israeli workers. From fruitpickers to bank managers, almost all workers in Israel are members. They and their families receive medical insurance, education, training, and many welfare benefits from the union. Histadrut also owns about a quarter of all Israeli businesses and is thus one of the country's largest employers.

Science and Technology

Research and development in science and technology play a major role in Israeli industry. Ten percent of Israel's national investment is spent on research, the highest figure of any industrialized country. Israel also produces the highest number of graduates in the sciences as a percentage of its population. Colleges such as the world-famous Haifa Technion specialize in science. Israeli scientists have pioneered advances in many fields, including electronics, scientific and medical equipment, computers, lasers, agriculture, and alternative energy. Techniques and equipment pioneered in Israel are now used around the world.

Fueled by this research, the manufacture of computer parts and scientific and electronic equipment are important industries. Other factories make chemicals, fertilizers, paper, plastics, textiles, clothing, and weapons and equipment for the military forces, including jet aircraft.

NATURAL RESOURCES

Israel's economic progress is remarkable in view of its scarcity of natural resources. Minerals, fuel, and water are all scarce. The few minerals that are present are found in the south and east, chiefly in the Dead Sea. The waters of the Dead Sea yield large quantities of potash, a mineral used to make fertilizers and pesticides. Dead Sea waters are also rich in bromine, which is used in industry, magnesium, and table salt.

ENERGY SOURCES

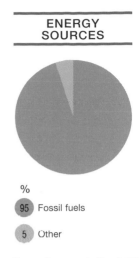

%
95 Fossil fuels

5 Other

Source: Government of Israel, 1996

Israel is dependent on foreign sources for its energy, a situation it is trying to remedy with the development of alternative energy sources.

Energy from the Sun

Israel does possess one natural resource in abundance: sunshine. Israeli scientists lead the world in the development of solar power. Solar panels are seen on most roofs, and three-quarters of Israeli homes are heated by solar power. There are also larger solar plants with giant curving mirrors that concentrate the Sun's rays to generate electricity.

The Environment

Since 1993–1994 was designated Environment Year, the Israeli government has been trying to promote recycling campaigns and the clean-up of rivers. Despite this, Israel faces ongoing problems. The diversion of water from the Jordan River for irrigation projects and the use of chemical fertilizers to "make the desert bloom" have severely disrupted Israel's ecology. Drainage has caused a drop in the levels of Lake Kinneret and the Dead Sea, both fed by the Jordan. The replanting of Israel's forests is a step in the right direction, but inevitably it is water that will prove the most valuable resource, both for nature and for the human population.

Other minerals are mined in the Negev Desert. They include phosphates, also used in fertilizer, and gypsum, used to make cement. Clay is mined for pottery, and copper is also found in small quantities. Limestone is quarried for building stone and ground up to make cement.

Israel has no coal and, unlike its neighbors, has only small amounts of oil and natural gas. There are no fast-flowing rivers that can be harnessed to generate electricity. So Israel must import almost all the fuel it needs for energy, mainly in the form of oil and coal. Crude oil is refined at Haifa and Ashdod. Israel has no nuclear power plants. In the future, it may be possible to extract oil from Israel's oil shale rocks.

Tourism in Israel, like the rest of the economy, is dominated by relations with the United States and Europe.

TOURISM

Tourism is a key industry in Israel, bringing in about $1 billion annually. Over two million tourists, mainly from western Europe and North America, arrive each year. Traditionally, tourists came to visit pilgrimage sites and ancient ruins, particularly in and around Jerusalem. However, Israel's warm, sunny climate is increasingly becoming one of the main attractions and tourism is enthusiastically promoted by the government. Tourists enjoy Israel's varied scenery, or relax in one of the country's resorts. The Dead Sea, Lake Kinneret, the Mediterranean coast, and Eilat are popular holiday destinations.

MAIN FOREIGN ARRIVALS

%

21	United States
11	United Kingdom
11	Germany
9	France
5	Russia
43	Others

Source: Government of Israel, 1997

TRANSPORTATION AND COMMUNICATION

Israel has a well-established transportation network. Its development was accelerated by the need to move Israel's armed forces and military equipment quickly to any part of the country. Paved roads now reach most areas. Nowadays, most middle-class families have an automobile. The average for the whole country is one automobile for every six people.

However, driving in Israel is not always a pleasurable experience. The country's roads are the most congested in the world, with an average of 160 automobiles for every mile (100 automobiles for every km) of road. This figure compares with 48 automobiles per mile (30 automobiles per km) in the United States and 94 per mile (59 per km) in Germany. Despite multilane highways, traffic jams are frequent on the most popular routes, and road accidents are also common—Israel has one of the

The city of Tel Aviv has grown so rapidly that its road system struggles to cope with growing traffic.

TRANSPORTATION

Israel's transportation system is largely centered, like its industry, in and around the cities of the Mediterranean coast. For individual travel, the bus system in Israel is much more efficient than the rail network, which often stops outside major cities. The West Bank is relatively poorly served by public transportation. Travel there is easiest by car.

——— major highways

+++++ railroads

- - - - canals

major airport

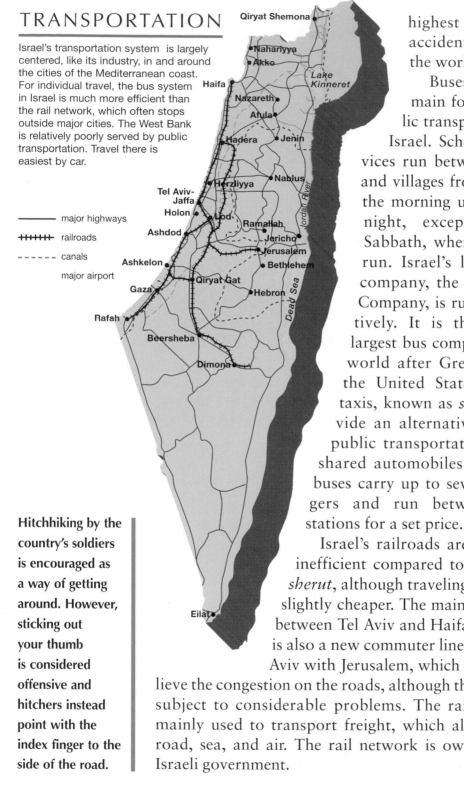

Hitchhiking by the country's soldiers is encouraged as a way of getting around. However, sticking out your thumb is considered offensive and hitchers instead point with the index finger to the side of the road.

highest traffic accident rates in the world.

Buses are the main form of public transportation in Israel. Scheduled services run between towns and villages from early in the morning until late at night, except on the Sabbath, when no buses run. Israel's largest bus company, the Egged Bus Company, is run cooperatively. It is the second-largest bus company in the world after Greyhound in the United States. Shared taxis, known as *sherut*, provide an alternative form of public transportation. These shared automobiles and mini-buses carry up to seven passengers and run between fixed stations for a set price.

Israel's railroads are slow and inefficient compared to buses and *sherut*, although traveling by train is slightly cheaper. The main rail link is between Tel Aviv and Haifa, but there is also a new commuter line linking Tel Aviv with Jerusalem, which helps to relieve the congestion on the roads, although this has been subject to considerable problems. The railroads are mainly used to transport freight, which also goes by road, sea, and air. The rail network is owned by the Israeli government.

Buses provide the main source of transportation in Israel's crowded cities, here in old Jerusalem.

Because it is surrounded by hostile neighbors, Israel's main transportation link with the outside world is by air. The main international airport is at Lod, near Tel Aviv, but there are also smaller airports at Atarot near Jerusalem and at Eilat. Israel's national airline, El Al, offers flights to destinations in Europe, North America, Africa, and elsewhere, and its extensive security procedures to counter airborne terrorism—traditionally a major threat in Israel—have been copied by airlines worldwide. The domestic airline, Arkia, operates short flights between Israel's largest cities and has recently begun to operate charter flights to and from foreign destinations. Many export goods, including fruit, flowers, and industrial products, leave the country by air.

Israel has three main deep-water ports: Haifa, Ashdod, and Eilat. Located on the Mediterranean, Haifa and Ashdod are gateways to Europe and the Americas. Eilat, on the Red Sea, serves the Middle East and Asia. The port at Jaffa serves as a gateway for agricultural produce. Inland, ferries on Lake Kinneret are popular with tourists.

Arts and Living

"In Israel it's enough to live—you don't have to do anything else, and you go to bed exhausted."

U.S. author Philip Roth

Israelis are a diverse people, with varied customs reflecting traditions in the 100-odd nations from which the Jews have immigrated during the last century. Israel's population is still growing and its culture is still changing, as thousands of new Jewish immigrants arrive each year from Africa, Asia, Europe, and the United States. In addition, Israel also has many non-Jewish citizens, mainly Arabs, with their own traditions, culture, and way of life.

In many ways, modern Israel's arts reflect this mixture, often developing strands of culture that have gone relatively unnoticed elsewhere. For example, the center of Tel Aviv has one of the finest collections of Bauhaus-influenced Modernist architecture in the world, largely built by German migrants during the 1930s. On the other hand the *sabrot*, the Israelis born in Israel, are anxious to explore their role as citizens of the Middle East. They see their country, situated between Africa and Asia, as reflecting the traditions of North Africa or Southwest Asia rather than those of Europe or the United States. Many of the *sabrot* feel an affinity with the Arab culture of the region in that it reflects a way of living more suited to the environment of the Middle East. This feeling is particularly strong among the young, where admiration for Arab culture is seen as a direct challenge to the more Western values of the older generation.

The attractions of Arab culture, such as this traditional market at the Damascus Gate in East Jerusalem, are increasingly recognized by younger Israelis.

FACT FILE

- Israel has one doctor for every 400 people. This compares with one for every 420 people in the United States and is one of the best doctor-patient ratios in the world.

- Israel's workforce of 2.3 million people is comprised of 60 percent men and 40 percent women. Of the women, 68 percent are mothers with children under 15.

- The United States has a Jewish community larger than Israel's entire Jewish population. In 1991, there were 5.5 million Jews in the United States, compared to 4.8 million in Israel.

THE ARTS IN ISRAEL

Israel is a young nation in which the arts are still evolving. However, the cultural traditions of Israel's inhabitants stretch back hundreds of years. Jewish immigrants from 100 different nations have brought the arts and culture of their former homelands to Israel. These mix with the distinctly Middle Eastern culture of the Arab population. Now a unique Israeli style is developing in many art forms, blending and building on the influence of many lands.

The Revival of Hebrew

Like Latin, Hebrew was regarded as a "dead" language 150 years ago. No one spoke it in everyday life, and it was used only in prayers, rituals, and in the Jewish holy texts. Today it is the national language of Israel.

The revival of Hebrew was initially the work of one man, a scholar named Eliezer Ben-Yehuda (1858–1922). He grew up in Lithuania in Eastern Europe, and emigrated to Israel in 1881. Once there, Ben-Yehuda declared that he and his family would speak only Hebrew. At first, his ideas were dismissed as crazy, but within decades, they had gained wide popular support. Ben-Yehuda wrote the first modern Hebrew dictionary and made up many new Hebrew words to describe modern objects and ideas.

Literature

Israel is a nation of book-lovers. Israelis buy books more regularly than the citizens of any other country except Iceland, the world's top book-buying nation. There are over 150 book publishers in Israel. Together, they produce more than 2,500 titles annually. Many books are published in Hebrew; others appear in different languages, including Arabic and Yiddish. The works of the world's best writers are also translated into Hebrew. Recently there has been a move away from Russian novelists, popular in the 1960s and 1970s, toward U.S. writers.

Every other year, Jerusalem hosts an international book fair. During Hebrew Book Week each spring, book stalls appear in parks and city squares. Jews are known as "the People of the Book," meaning the world's most influential book, the Bible. The phrase is apt in a modern sense of Israelis today as well.

Novelist Shmuel Yosef Agnon (1888–1970) is one of Israel's best-known writers. He won the Nobel Prize for Literature in 1960. Other famous writers include Chaim Nachman Bialik (1873–1934), Max Brod (1884–1968), and Amos Oz (born 1939). The work of humorist Ephraim Kishon (born 1924) is well-known abroad. Israel has many popular poets, too, including Yehuda Amichai and Natan Zach.

Theater and film

Going to the theater is a popular pastime in Israel. There are many theater companies, including children's and puppet theater groups, and street theaters. Israel's national theater company is called Habimah, which simply means "the stage." The company was formed in Moscow in 1917 and moved to Tel Aviv in 1932.

Theaters in Israel perform plays by international writers and Israeli playwrights, who include Hanoch Levine and Yehoshua Sobol. Plays are performed in Hebrew, Arabic, and other languages. The town of

The actor Haim Topol in the film version of **Fiddler on the Roof.**

The Israel Philharmonic Orchestra performs at the opening of the Jerusalem City Museum at the Jaffa Gate in Jerusalem.

Akko on the northern coast hosts an alternative theater festival each year. Israel's film industry is also growing. Acclaimed Israeli actors include Haim Topol, Uri Zohar, and Oded Kotler.

Music

Every large city in Israel and many small towns and kibbutzim have their own concert hall. Israel has six major orchestras, including the Israel Philharmonic Orchestra and the Jerusalem Symphony Orchestra. There are many smaller chamber orchestras too.

Israel has produced many great musicians. Violinist Yitzhak Perlman (born 1945), pianist and conductor Daniel Barenboim (born 1942), and conductor Zubin Mehta (born 1936) trained in Israel and have gone on to win international fame. The country hosts many music festivals, including the Israel Festival in Jerusalem, the Zimriya Choirs Festival, and the festival at Kibbutz Ein Gev. Competitions for instruments such as the piano, cello, and harp show the skills of Israel's finest musicians.

Many different styles of folk music are enjoyed in Israel. Immigrants from Europe, the Middle East, and North Africa have all brought a rich musical heritage with them. Many folk styles are popular, including *klezmer*, a folk music that originated in Eastern Europe and features the violin and clarinet. Greek music is also very popular in Israel. Now all these influences are blending to produce a distinctively Israeli sound. Rock, pop, and jazz music are also popular, particularly among young people.

A woman dances at a Moroccan Jewish celebration in Jerusalem.

Dance

Dance is another popular art form in Israel. There are several companies performing classical ballet such as Israel Ballet. Modern dance groups include Bat Dor, the Kibbutz Dance group, and the Inbal Dance Theater, which blends classical ballet with folk dancing from Yemen, where there was a large Jewish population. *Kol Demama*, which means "Voice of Silence," is an innovative dance troupe that employs deaf and hearing dancers. Deaf dancers keep time to the music by sensing the vibrations of the other dancers' feet through the floor. Folk dancing is a popular pastime among Israelis of all ages, Jews and Arabs alike. Cities, towns, and most kibbutzim have their own folk dance troupes.

Painting and sculpture

The visual arts are growing and developing in Israel. Well-known painters include Yakov Agam (born 1928), Menashe Kadishman (born 1932), and Avigdor Arikha (born 1928). Many of Schmuel Bak's (born 1933) paintings refer to his experience of the Holocaust in Lithuania. These artists' work sells well both at home and abroad. Tel Aviv, Jaffa, Safed, and other major cities have museums and galleries which display the best modern art. There is also an artists' village at Ein Hod near Haifa.

Israel is famous for silverwork, jewelry-making, glassware, ceramics, and weaving. Craft fairs held in Jerusalem and Jaffa each year attract deal-ers, art-lovers, and tourists alike.

Israeli artist Schmuel Bak's paintings refer indirectly to his experience of the Holocaust to convey "an enormous effort to put everything together, when it is impossible...because the broken things can never be made whole again."

The media

Israel has a good communications network, with two dozen daily newspapers. Thirteen are in Hebrew, including *Ma'ariv* and *Ha'aretz*, while the remainder are in Arabic, Yiddish, or other languages. *Ha'aretz* is also available in an English-language edition. The largest-selling Arabic daily is *Al-Quds*. *The Jerusalem Post* is the only daily newspaper published exclusively in English.

The Israel Broadcasting Authority operates two TV channels and several radio stations. They broadcast a variety of programs in Hebrew, Arabic, and other languages. In addition, there is a cable TV network and many independent radio stations. Most families in Israel own a TV set and at least one radio.

DAILY LIFE

Israelis are a hard-working and creative people who traditionally have been drawn together by the need to build the nation of Israel. Despite a good degree of independence, the people are supported by a large and powerful state that controls many areas of public life. Levels of education are high and historically there has been a strong sense of community, although this has declined in recent years as the country has become wealthier.

Town and Country

Less than 10 percent of Israelis live in rural areas. Nine out of every ten Israelis live in towns and cities, mainly in tall apartment buildings. Over one-quarter of the population lives in the largest three cities: Jerusalem, Tel Aviv, and Haifa. Tens of thousands more live in smaller centers, including new "development towns."

Development towns are settlements that have been built since the 1950s to relieve overcrowding in the largest cities. Karmiel and Qiryat Shemona in the north and Arad and Dimona in the Negev are all development towns. Since 1967, a number of Jewish settlements have also been founded in the occupied West Bank. This has caused considerable hostility between Jews and Palestinians.

In rural areas, around half of the population lives either communally or cooperatively, sharing the products of their work in kibbutzim. The first kibbutz was founded at Degania on the Jordan River in 1909. Now there are 250 kibbutzim

Coming to Israel

Since Israel passed its main immigration law, called the Law of Return, in 1950, millions of Jewish immigrants have settled in the country. According to the Law of Return, anyone of Jewish descent is officially welcome. Since the 1970s, large waves of immigrants have arrived from Eastern Europe, the Middle East, North Africa, and the former Soviet Union. In the 1980s and early 1990s, a total of 30,000 Ethiopian Jews, known as Falashas, were brought to Israel in a series of airlifts codenamed "Operation Moses." The Falashas claim to have been descended from King Solomon.

The first few months are hard for many of the newcomers. The immigrants must learn to adjust to a new society where customs may be very different from in their former homelands. In addition, they must learn the Hebrew language, find a place to live, and get a job. The Israeli government offers support in all these areas. All new immigrants attend *ulpan*, or language school, for an intensive five-month course of instruction in Hebrew and Jewish culture.

The Jewish settlement at Kiryat Arba near Hebron has been a controversial one. The decision by Jews to occupy Hebron's old hospital there led to violent confrontations between Arabs and Jews.

The word for Sabbath (shabat) written in the Hebrew script.

scattered throughout the country. Many leading Israelis have been kibbutzniks (kibbutz-dwellers). The motto of the kibbutzim is a classically egalitarian one: "From each according to his abilities, to each according to his needs." Not all kibbutzim are farms. In some, manufacturing or tourism is the main money-earner. Most kibbutzim now have a swimming pool and other sports facilities, a library, and a concert hall or museum.

RELIGION

In Israel, everyone is free to practice his or her religion. Around 80 percent of the population are Jewish. About 14 percent are Muslim, over 3 percent are Christian, and of the remaining 2 percent many are Druze, a Muslim sect. The dominant Jewish religion is linked with many national events and holidays, although the state is officially secular (nonreligious). The Jewish Sabbath, Saturday, is the main day of rest in Israel. Shops, offices, and public transportation close down from sunset on Friday, when the Sabbath starts, to sunset on Saturday, when it ends. On Friday evening, the holy day begins with the lighting of candles, blessings, and a special family meal.

Judaism

The guiding principles of the Jewish religion are the 613 *mitzvot*, or commandments, set down in the Torah—the first five books of the Bible. Over the centuries, these laws have been interpreted by generations of Jewish rabbis (scholars). The Talmud is the main book of commentary on the law. The Jewish or Hebrew Bible is roughly equivalent to the Old Testament of the Christian Bible, although the Old Testament includes some books not recognized by the Jewish tradition.

Of Israel's Jews, only about 20 percent are Orthodox, which means they observe traditional religious law strictly. Another 60 percent observe some Jewish customs and laws, for example, those regarding food and cooking. The remaining 20 percent are secular, or nonreligious. Hasidim are very devout Orthodox Jews whose origins lie in 18th-century Poland. Hasidic men are distinguished by their long beards and sidelocks, and black coats and hats. Hasidic women dress very modestly; the married women cover their heads with a scarf or wig.

Orthodox Jews hold up the scrolls of the Torah, containing the first five books of the Bible, the most sacred of Jewish texts.

Jewish Festivals

For Jews, the religious year begins in autumn, with Rosh Hashanah, the New Year festival, falling in September or October. Ten days later, Yom Kippur, the Day of Atonement, is the Jews' most holy day. Some Jews fast for the whole day and ask God to forgive their sins during the previous year.

Sukkot, the feast of Tabernacles, falls in October. Jews build shelters where they eat and sleep to remember

The Jewish Calendar

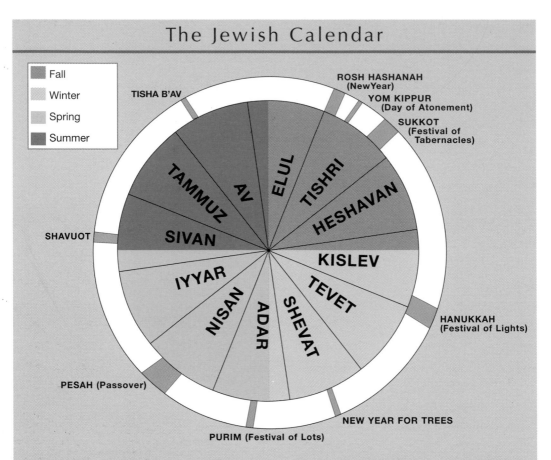

Fall
Winter
Spring
Summer

TISHA B'AV

ROSH HASHANAH
(New Year)

YOM KIPPUR
(Day of Atonement)

SUKKOT
(Festival of
Tabernacles)

TAMMUZ
AV
ELUL
TISHRI
HESHAVAN
SIVAN
KISLEV
IYYAR
TEVET
NISAN
ADAR
SHEVAT

SHAVUOT

HANUKKAH
(Festival of Lights)

PESAH (Passover)

NEW YEAR FOR TREES

PURIM (Festival of Lots)

The Jewish calendar has remained unchanged since about A.D. 900 and is the official calendar of the state of Israel. The starting point of Hebrew history is the year 3761 B.C., the traditional date of the creation of the world as deduced from the Hebrew Bible. So the year beginning in the autumn of 2000 is 5761 in the Jewish calendar. The Jewish calendar is based on the cycles of the moon and consists of lunar months alternating between 29 and 30 days. An extra month is put in seven times every 19 years to keep the calendar consistent with the solar year.

The Jewish festivals are concentrated in the spring and fall and were originally linked to the agricultural seasons of the year. So, for example, the festival of Sukkot in fall was linked to an annual pilgrimage to Jerusalem at harvesttime. Pesah or Passover, while celebrating the liberation of the Hebrews from slavery in Egypt, was also linked to the promise of new life heralded by the spring. In addition to the religious festivals, Israel commemorates Holocaust Remembrance Day on the 27th day of Nisan and Independence Day on the fifth day of Iyyar.

the ancient Israelites who spent 40 years wandering in the desert after Moses led them out of Egypt.

In December, Hanukkah is the festival of lights, held as the Christian Christmas approaches. It celebrates the victory of the Hebrews under Judas Maccabeus, called Maccabees, over Palestine's Greek rulers in 167 B.C., and the recapture of the temple. According to the Talmud (see p.103), during this time one day's supply of oil burned miraculously in the temple for eight days. On each day of Hanukkah people light a candle on the traditional eight-branched candlestick called a menorah, and give presents.

Purim is a joyous festival that falls in February or March and celebrates the deliverance of the Jews from oppression. Children and adults wear fancy dress, have fun, and give one another presents. Later in spring, Passover (Pesah) is a seven-day festival that commemorates the Exodus—the ancient Israelites' delivery from slavery in Egypt around 1250 B.C. During Passover, Jews eat *matza* (unleavened bread) instead of ordinary bread. The festival ends with a special meal called the *seder*, with readings from the Exodus story. Christian holy week, ending in Easter, falls around the same time. The festival of Shavuot in June celebrates God's gift to the Hebrews of the Ten Commandments. Tisha b'Av in July commemorates the destruction of the temple in Jerusalem.

The month of May sees three nonreligious national holidays. On Holocaust Remembrance Day, people remember all the Jews who were killed by the Nazis during World War II (see p. 69).

שלום

The word shalom, *here written in the Hebrew script, has three meanings—hello, goodbye, and peace.*

Although the festival of Purim has its origins in the book of Esther in the Bible, religion plays a small part in the celebrations.

Remembrance Day honors Israel's soldiers who have died in war, and Independence Day celebrates the birth of the nation.

Islam

Muslims follow the religion of Islam, a belief system founded by the prophet Mohammed in the seventh century in what is now Saudi Arabia. Islam means obedience to God and the religion is based on the teachings of the Koran, the Islamic holy book, which is believed to have been revealed to the prophet Mohammed by God. Muslims follow strict laws regarding dress, food, and the mixing of the sexes. In Israel almost all Muslims are Arabs whose ancestors have lived in the land for more than a thousand years. Their mosques and holy places are largely to be found in the occupied territories of the West Bank, Gaza, the Golan, and East Jerusalem, the most important of these is the Dome of the Rock in Jerusalem.

For Muslims, the most important religious festival is Ramadan, which occurs in the ninth month of the Muslim year. Muslims fast between the hours of sunrise and sunset for the whole month. The festival ends with a three-day celebration called *Id al-fitr*.

Food and Drink

Israel's cuisine comes from many countries, like its people. The nation's favorite dishes reflect the cooking of northern Europe, the Mediterranean, and the Middle East. European dishes include borscht (beet soup), chicken soup, and chopped chicken liver. Other dishes originated in the Middle East. *Bourekas* are flaky pastries filled with tasty cheese, spinach, or spiced potato. *Kunafa* and *sambusak* are Arab delicacies, puff pastries with a sweet or tasty filling.

Israelis enjoy their food, and like plenty of it. The day is punctuated with meals and snacks. Breakfast may consist simply of a heaped plate of salad, with sliced green peppers, radishes, and carrots, topped with salty cheese. A few hours later, the "ten o'clock meal" is a snack of tea with biscuits or a sandwich, followed by lunch. Late in the afternoon, the "four o'clock meal" may be a drink and another sandwich, to stave off hunger pangs until supper in the early evening. *Beteyaron* is a Hebrew word meaning "Enjoy your meal!"

As in most Western nations, Israelis now buy much of their food at supermarkets, which are stocked with a variety of international products as well as home-

During the Passover meal Jews eat foods that remind them of the Israelites' escape from Egypt. These include flat bread or wafers and bitter herbs to remind them of slavery.

Vines have existed in Israel since 3000 B.C. The main vine-growing areas are now located near Mount Carmel and in the Golan Heights.

grown food. Fruit and vegetables are often bought at market, where stalls are piled high with local produce. When eating out in cities such as Tel Aviv, Israelis choose between a wide range of restaurants, offering cooking styles from around the world. Many, however, prefer to eat "on the go," buying a snack from one of the fast-food stands that line the streets.

Falafel is one of the most popular snack foods in Israel—fried balls of chickpeas served with onions, garlic, and a spicy sauce. Often they are wrapped in a "pocket" of flat pita bread with salad, and smothered with tahini, a paste made from sesame seeds.

Falafel

Falafel is sold on street corners in every city and town in Israel. It is the most popular fast food and is eaten served in pita bread with salad or as individual balls dipped in relish or hummus.

Serves four people

1lb (454g) can of chickpeas (drained) or fresh chickpeas (soaked for 24 hours)
$1/2$ to 1 cup of breadcrumbs or fine bulgar (crushed wheat)
1 large onion chopped
1 tbs. finely chopped parsley
1 tsp. ground coriander or cumin
1 tsp. dried hot red peppers
1 egg
1 tsp. salt
1 tsp. garlic powder
Vegetable oil for frying
Mixed salad and pita bread for serving

Mix the chickpeas with the onion. Add parsley, lightly beaten egg, and spices. Chop in a blender. Add the breadcrumbs and blend again until the mixture begins to form a solid mass. Make small balls about one inch (2.5 cm) in diameter and flatten them into patties. Heat the oil and fry the patties until golden brown on both sides. Remove from the frying pan and drain off the oil on paper towels.

Kosher Foods

In many Orthodox Jewish households in Israel, as in Orthodox Jewish communities elsewhere, dietary laws (*kashrut*) from the Bible govern the preparation of food and which foods can be eaten. Kosher (meaning "proper") foods are all foods that are "ritually correct." According to these laws, no forms of pig meat or shellfish must ever be eaten. Dairy and meat products may not be prepared or eaten together. This means, for example, that milk cannot be added to coffee after a meal involving meat. Meat must be from animals slaughtered according to religious ritual. Kosher animals are those that have cloven hooves and live on a diet of grass or plant leaves.

Most hotels and restaurants in Israel serve only kosher foods, though some cater to non-Jewish tourists. Muslims have their own set of dietary laws that control how food is prepared. Like Jews, Muslims are forbidden to eat pork.

Chickpeas are also the main ingredients in a tasty paté called hummus. Both of these delicious and healthy foods are Middle Eastern in origin.

Other snacks available from street stands include *shwarma*, grilled slices of lamb served in pita bread, tender corn-on-the-cob, and dried fruit. These are washed down with freshly squeezed fruit juice from a street vendor. *Garinim*, the Israeli equivalent of potato chips, are also sold on the streets. They are salty, roasted seeds, sometimes mixed with cashews, almonds, and pistachios.

Out in the countryside, roadside stands sell local produce such as plump, red strawberries and ripe melons to passing travelers. The little stands are strung with lights, so business can continue late into the night.

Chicken, turkey, lamb, and fish such as trout and sea bass are all popular foods in Israel. Dairy products include a wide variety of cheeses made from goat's, sheep's, or cow's milk, as well as yogurt and sour cream. Salads accompany most meals in Israel. Beer, wine, Turkish coffee, and soda are popular drinks. Many festivals are linked with special foods through traditions that have been brought from other countries.

The dietary requirements of both Orthodox Jews and Muslims, combined with the abundance of fresh fruit and vegetables, make Israel a vegetarian's paradise.

HEALTH

A century ago, health standards in Palestine were poor. Now Israel's health care is among the finest in the world. Over 300 hospitals offer general and specialized care to patients. Most hospitals are run by the government or local authority, but some are owned privately or run by charities or religious groups. A network of health clinics and 900 mother-and-child centers covers the whole country. Israel has a higher number of doctors for its population than almost any country in the world. Many dangerous diseases, such as malaria, carried by mosquitoes, have now been brought under control.

Israeli women live to an average age of 80, men to 76. At 78, Israel's average life expectancy rate is among the highest in the world. Most

Therapeutic Mud

The waters of the Dead Sea contain 20 times as much bromine (a relaxant), 15 times as much magnesium (which clears skin allergies), and ten times as much iodine as normal water. The water and the mud of the Dead Sea beaches is supposed to be good for the skin. A large cosmetics industry has grown up, creating products that exploit the Dead Sea's properties.

people take out health insurance to cover medical care. There are four major insurance programs, including one run by Histadrut.

Magen David Adom (the Red Shield of David) is Israel's emergency medical service, the equivalent of the Red Cross. This organization runs the ambulance service, a network of first-aid stations, and the nation's blood donor program. In a country that has spent much of its short history at war, Israeli doctors have become expert at treating all kinds of emergency injuries, including burns caused by bomb attacks. Israeli scientists and technicians have pioneered advances in many fields of medicine, including heart, brain, and eye surgery, cancer research, and bone disease treatment.

EDUCATION

Israel is justly proud of its school system. Education has been a priority from Israel's earliest years, and one of the country's first laws established free schooling for all children between the ages of 5 and 14. Now school is free for children up to 18, and compulsory until the age of 16. Israel currently spends 6 percent of its gross national product on education—a high proportion compared to many developed nations.

Most young children of 3 and 4 attend nursery school or some form of pre-school, for which their parents pay. Free education begins with kindergarten around the age of 5. Six years of primary education and six years of high school follow. Senior high school students specialize in humanities, science, agriculture, or military studies. Between the ages of 5 and 13, children go to school between 8:00 A.M. and 1:00 P.M. For high school students, schools lasts until 2:00 P.M. There is no school on Saturday, the Sabbath.

Israeli schools cater to children from a variety of different religious backgrounds. There are separate schools for Jewish, Arab, and Druze children. Arab and Druze schools include study of the history and culture

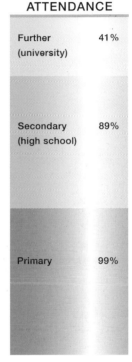

EDUCATIONAL ATTENDANCE

Further (university)	41%
Secondary (high school)	89%
Primary	99%

Source: Encyclopedia Britannica

Educational standards are very high in Israel, and a good proportion of students go on to further education. Despite high standards at home, many Israelis also go on to study abroad, usually either in Europe or the United States.

of Arab peoples. Students learn in Arabic and receive religious instruction in Islam, the Druze religion, or Christianity.

There are three main types of Jewish schools. Public schools offer a general education with some religious studies. Public religious schools focus more on Jewish

Bar Mitzvah

Bar Mitzvah is the ceremony in Judaism in which a boy becomes an adult—at the age of 13—and takes on the duties or commandments (*mitzvot*, plural of *mitzvah*) outlined in the Bible. The boy is initiated into the adult religious community by putting on the *tallit* (the prayer shawl) and reading from the Torah (the first five books of the Bible, *see* the image above) and the *haftarah* (the books of the Prophets) in the synagogue. This usually occurs during a Sabbath service on or before the boy's 13th birthday. More modern synagogues also now perform a similar ceremony for girls at 12. In addition to the religious ceremony, the young man is also given presents and there is a celebratory family meal.

How to Say...

Modern Hebrew is derived from the ancient language of the Hebrew Bible and was revived in the late-19th century. Many new phrases have been coined in the last 100 years, and there have even been some borrowings from Arabic. Many other languages are heard in Israel, including Arabic, Russian, German, and English, but Hebrew is the national tongue. Below are a few Hebrew words and phrases that may be useful should you ever visit Israel. The translations into Hebrew are only approximate as the words would normally be written in the Hebrew script.

Please   *Bevakasha*

Thank you   *Toda*

Yes   *Ken*

No   *Lo*

Hello   *Shalom*

Goodbye   *Shalom*

See you later   *Lehitraot*

Good morning   *Boker tov*

Good afternoon   *Shalom*

Good night   *Layla tov*

How are you?
   (masculine) *Ma shlomka?*
   (feminine) *ma shlomekh?*
   How's life?   *Eykh hainyanim?*

Fine   *Beseder*

Sorry   *Sliha*

Excuse me   *Sliha*

I understand   (masculine) *Ani mevin*
   (feminine) *ani mevina*

I don't understand   (masculine) *Eyneni mevin*, (feminine) *eyneni mevina*

Do you speak English?   *Ata medaber anglit?*

What is your name?
   (masculine) *Ma shimka?*
   (feminine) *ma shmekh?*

My name is... *Shmi...*

You're welcome   *Al lo davar*

Sir/Mr.   *Mar*

Madam/Mrs.   *Gveret*

Miss   *Gveret*

Numbers:

One   *Ehad*

Two   *Shnayim*

Three   *Shlosha*

Four   *Arbaa*

Five   *Hamisha*

Six   *Shisha*

Seven   *Shiva*

Eight   *Shmona*

Nine   *Tisha*

Ten   *Asara*

Days of the week:

Sunday   *Yom rishon*

Monday   *Yom sheni*

Tuesday   *Yom shlishi*

Wednesday   *Yom revii*

Thursday   *Yom hamishi*

Friday   *Yom shishi*

Saturday   *Shabat*

National Service

Israel is still officially at war with some of its neighbors and therefore maintains a large defense force. Both men and women must enter military service at the age of 18, men for three years, women for 18 months. After this initial phase, everyone is assigned to a reserve unit from which they are recalled to do about 30 days of service a year until the age of 35 (or in the case of women, seldom after 25). Israel takes national security issues very seriously. A soldier who loses a rifle can be imprisoned for seven years; as a result many are to be seen carrying them around off duty. The role of women soldiers in the Israeli army has led to a far more prominent role for women in Israeli society despite the male-biased nature of the traditional Middle East.

religious studies. There are also independent religious schools, not funded by the government, which offer intensive study of the Orthodox Jewish religion as well as a basic grounding in other subjects.

Israel's higher education system is also well developed. Around 41 percent of all young people receive some form of higher education. This compares with 58 percent in the United States. But young people go to college later in Israel than in America, after they have completed their military service between the ages of 18 and 21.

Israel has eight universities, including the Hebrew University of Jerusalem, Tel Aviv and Haifa Universities, the internationally famous Weizmann Institute of Science, and the Open University. In addition, there are also many colleges that offer courses in technology, agriculture, music, fashion, art, physical education, and teacher training.

SPORT AND LEISURE

In the evenings and on weekends Israelis meet with friends and family to share a meal, laugh, and talk. For some, leisure time is still partly structured around religion and historical traditions brought from other countries. But there is also an element in Israeli society that has embraced wholeheartedly the culture to be found in the United States and western Europe. Like people elsewhere, Israelis go dancing, make music, or just

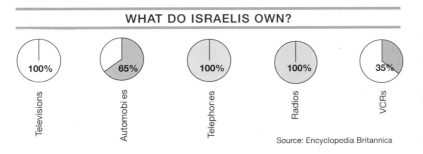

WHAT DO ISRAELIS OWN?

100%	65%	100%	100%	35%
Televisions	Automobiles	Telephones	Radios	VCRs

Source: Encyclopedia Britannica

Although most Israelis enjoy a good standard of living, levels of ownership of luxury goods still falls below those in Europe and North America.

relax in front of the TV or radio. Concerts, films, and plays are highly popular. Many Israelis benefit from speaking both English and Hebrew, so plays are often performed in English. Israelis love reading. Books, magazines, or newspapers play an important role in Israeli life.

Israel is also a country of outdoor activities: hiking, jogging, horseback riding, and camping are all popular. Most Israelis live within reach of the sea and in their free time they head down to the beach for games such as volleyball or *matkot*, a bat-and-ball game, or for watersports such as swimming, snorkeling, windsurfing, sailing, and scuba diving.

Soccer and basketball are the most popular sports in Israel. The national soccer team trains at Ramat Gan stadium in Tel Aviv, which houses 45,000 spectators. Israel has come close to qualifying for the European Championship but has so far been unsuccessful. There is a highly competitive domestic league. The three major teams are Maccabi Tel Aviv, followed by Beitar Jerusalem, and Maccabi Haifa. In basketball Israel is represented in the European League by Maccabi Tel Aviv, which won the championship in 1977 and 1980. Hapoel Jerusalem is another successful Israeli team. Running is another popular sport, and Jerusalem has its own running club.

Tennis, badminton, athletics, and gymnastics are all other sports in which Israelis have excelled in recent years. Every four years, Jewish athletes from all over the world arrive to compete in the Maccabiah Games—Israel's equivalent of the Olympic Games.

HOW ISRAELIS SPEND THEIR MONEY

%
- 22.6 Housing
- 21.8 Food and drink
- 13.2 Clothing and household goods
- 4.1 Transportation
- 4 Energy
- 34.3 Other

Source: Encyclopedia Britannica

The basics of life are still expensive in Israel and relatively little is spent on leisure.

The Future

"We, like you, are people—people who want to build a home, plant a tree, to love, to live...as human beings, as free men."

Yitzhak Rabin on signing the Israeli–Palestinian Declaration

Israel's future is hard to predict, especially since it is a relatively new country with a diverse population and unstable history. Overall, living standards are high, and in recent times, there have been fewer wars for Israel compared with the constant conflict of the nation's first three decades. However, much of Israel's future stability still depends on its Arab neighbors. Changes of regime in any one of these surrounding, often hostile, countries can bring hope or despair to Israel. Public opinion has recently seemed to accept that some sort of compromise with the Palestinians is inevitable, as is the return of the Golan Heights to Syria. More contentious though is the matter of who rules Jerusalem: both the Israelis and the Palestinians claim it as their capital, and so far neither seems willing to share sovereignty with the other.

THE BOOMING ECONOMY

One of Israel's greatest successes has been economic. A small nation that began with few natural resources, Israel has become the economic powerhouse of the region, with an economy approximately the size of those of Egypt, Syria, and Jordan combined. The country's early emphasis on education, social services, and building its transportation and infrastructure, together with the immigration of skilled professionals from all

The holy sites of the Dome of the Rock, holy site of Islam (background), and the Wailing Wall (center), sacred to Jews, lie at the root of disputes over Jerusalem.

over the world, has led to a highly competitive economy based on trade with the United States and Europe. However, Israel is still heavily dependent on the United States, so that a change in policy by the U.S. government could have serious consequences. At the end of the 20th century, the United States seemed less concerned than in the past about Israel maintaining supremacy in the Middle East and it could cut its economic and military aid to Israel in the future. Jewish influence in U.S. political life is large, however, and several U.S. presidents have attempted to secure their place in history by brokering a peace deal in the region.

The Wye Agreement

Israel signed a new U.S.-backed peace accord with the Palestinians in October 1998 called the Wye Agreement. Under its terms, Israel began further troop withdrawals from the West Bank and the first Palestinian airport was opened in the Gaza Strip. The Palestinian Authority also established its base at Gaza City. However, the accord was severely hampered by the actions of Jewish settlers and the implicit support they received from Benjamin Netanyahu's government.

THE PROCESS STALLS

Peace developements were beset with difficulties during Benjamin Netanyahu's term of government. Netanyahu suspended the terms of the peace accord and encouraged the settlement of Jews in previously Arab areas. There were complaints too that Yasser Arafat had done too little to counteract Palestinian terrorism that originated within the territory controlled by the Palestinian Authority. Threats by Arafat to declare an independent Palestinian state unilaterally (without the support of Israel and other nations) may increase tension in the area if followed through.

Renewed hope

In the general election held in May 1999, Benjamin Netanyahu's conservative coalition was overwhelmingly defeated by Ehud Barak and the Israeli Labor Party in coalition with other parties under the banner of One

Israel. This gave many people hope that the change of government would breathe new life into the flagging peace process. The two parties met at Camp David in the summer of 2000, but no new accord was reached, largely because both sides wish to control East Jerusalem and the sacred sites of the Old City.

A VISION OF THE FUTURE

If the peace process is successful, Israel may be able to cut its vast defense budget, which stood at around $6.6 billion in the late 1990s. This would clearly provide a huge boost to the economy. There is also no longer a boycott on Israeli goods by members of the Arab League, with the result that new markets have opened up. Tourism has increased since the 1991 Persian Gulf War. In the end, the promise of economic development and of a higher standard of living may convince all sides that they need to approach the negotiating table.

The New Realism

There is an increasing acceptance among the Arab nations that the state of Israel is a reality and that with the enormous financial and military support of the United States, Israel cannot be destroyed. On the Israeli side there is a growing acceptance that the occupied territories of the West Bank and the Golan Heights cannot be held indefinitely and that Israel's future security and economic prosperity depend on reaching a peace accord with its Arab neighbors, particularly Syria. The benefits for both sides would be enormous. For Israel, economic dominance of the region is virtually assured. For Jordan the establishment of a Palestinian homeland on the West Bank would be a major achievement for its large Palestinian population. For Syria, peace with Israel would ensure the return of the Golan Heights and end the costly war in Lebanon. At the time of writing, these difficulties remain to be resolved and the world still awaits a breakthrough.

At the end of 1998 there were 216 Jewish Israeli settlements in the West Bank, 42 in the Golan Heights, 24 in Gaza, and 29 in East Jerusalem.

Almanac

POLITICAL

Country name:
Official long form: State of Israel
Short form: Israel
Local long form: *Medinat Yisra'el*
Local short form: *Yisra'el*

Nationality:
> noun: Israeli (s)
> adjective: Israeli

Official languages: Hebrew and Arabic

Capital city: Jerusalem

Type of government: parliamentary
democracy

Suffrage (voting rights): 18 years and
over, universal

National anthem: "Hatikyah"
("Hope")

National holiday: 5 Iyyar (*see* p. 104
for Jewish calendar)

Flag:

GEOGRAPHICAL

Location: Middle East, bordering the
Mediterranean; latitudes 31°
30 north and longitudes
34° 45 east

Climate: On the coastal plain summers
are humid and winters wet; in
the hill regions summers are
warm and winters cold. In the
southern and eastern desert
areas it is hot and dry all year.

Total area: 8,017 square miles
(20,770 sq. km)
land: 98%
water: 2%

Coastline: 170 miles (273 km)

Terrain: desert in the south and east,
a low coastal plain in the west,
mountains in the east

Highest point: Mount Meron,
3,963 feet (1,208 m)
Lowest point: Dead Sea,
-1,312 feet (-400 m)

Natural resources: copper, phosphates,
bromide, potash, clay, sand,
sulfur, manganese, gas, oil

Land use: arable land 17%
forests and woodland 6%
permanent crops 4%
permanent pasture 7%
other: 66%

Natural hazards: sandstorms

POPULATION

Population: (1999 est.) 5.7 million

Population density: 699 people per square mile (269 per sq. km)

Population growth rate: 1.81%

Birthrate (1999 est.): 19.83 births per 1,000 of the population

Death rate (1999 est.): 6.16 deaths per 1,000 of the population

Sex ratio (1999 est.): 99 males per 100 females

Total fertility rate (1999 est.): 2.68 per woman in the population

Infant mortality rate (1999 est.): 7.78 deaths per 1,000 live births

Life expectancy at birth (1999 est.): total population: 78.61 years
male: 76.7 years
female: 80.61 years

Literacy:
total population: 95%
male: 97%
female: 93%

ECONOMY

Currency: new Israeli shekel (NIS); 1 NIS= 100 new agorot

Exchange rate (1999): $1 = NIS 4.16

Gross national product (1999): $94.4 billion (37th-largest economy in the world)

Average annual growth rate (1990–1997): 5.8%

GNP per capita (1999 est.): $16,180

Average annual inflation rate (1998): 5.4%

Unemployment rate (1998 est.): 8.7%

Exports (1998): $35 billion
Imports (1998): $43.2 billion

Foreign aid received (1996): $1.24 billion

Human Development Index
(an index scaled from 0 to 100 combining statistics indicating adult literacy, years of schooling, life expectancy, and income levels):
80.9 (U.S. 94.3)

TIME LINE—ISRAEL

World History

**Palestinian/
Israeli History**

c. 50,000 B.C.

c. **40,000** Modern humans—*Homo sapiens sapiens*—emerge.

c. 10,000 B.C.

c. **8000** B.C. Agriculture develops in Western Asia.

3000–1000 B.C. Height of ancient Egyptian civilization.

c. **10,000** B.C. Neolithic humans settle the Jordan Valley and the Mediterranean coast.

3000 B.C. Canaanite city kingdoms develop.

c. **2000** B.C. Abraham settles in Canaan.

c. 1050 B.C.

1200–1000 B.C. Phoenicians rise to power in the Mediterranean.

753 B.C. City of Rome founded.

332 B.C. Alexander the Great creates Greek empire.

1030–586 B.C. Israelites inhabit Palestine.

586–538 B.C. Babylonians rule Palestine.

538–332 B.C. Persians rule Palestine.

1792–1815 Napoleonic Wars in Europe.

1750–1850 Industrial Revolution in the West.

1526 Foundation of Mughal empire.

1288 Ottoman state founded in Turkey.

1065 Start of the Crusades.

c. **570–632** Life of Prophet Mohammed.

A.D. 98–117 Roman empire reaches its greatest extent.

146 B.C. Greece comes under Roman rule.

1799 Napoleon seizes part of Palestine.

1517–1917 Ottoman Turks rule Palestine.

c. 1500

1187–1516 Muslim Arabs rule Palestine.

1100–1187 Crusaders rule Kingdom of Jerusalem.

640–1099 Muslim Arabs rule Palestine.

A.D. 323–614 Christian Romans rule Palestine.

A.D. 300

5 B.C.–C. A.D. 30 Life of Jesus Christ.

63 B.C.–A.D. 323 Pagan Romans rule Palestine.

166–63 B.C. Maccabean Jews rule Palestine.

332–166 B.C. Greeks rule Palestine.

c. 300 B.C.

c.1850

1897 First Zionist conference.

1914–1918 World War I.

1917 Balfour Declaration.

1933 Nazis come to power in Germany.

1939–1945 World War II.

1880–1903 First wave of Jewish immigration.

1918–1948 British rule Palestine.

1947 UN votes to split Palestine into Jewish and Arab states.

1948–1949 Foundation of the state of Israel, leading to War of Independence.

2000 The West celebrates the Millennium—2,000 years since the birth of Christ.

1999 Kosovo conflict in Europe.

2000 Israeli-Palestinian talks at Camp David fail to reach new agreement.

1999 Return of Labor coalition to power leads to hopes of renewed peace process.

1998 Wye River Agreement. Israel agrees to further withdrawals from the West Bank.

1995–1997 Israel withdraws from Arab areas of the West Bank.

1994 Israel signs peace deal with Jordan.

1993 Israeli-Palestinian peace deal (the Oslo Accords) signed.

c.1950

1962 Cuban Missile Crisis.

1963–1975 Vietnam War.

1969 First man lands on the moon.

1973–1974 World Oil Crisis.

1979 Iranian Revolution.

Late 1970s Rise of Islamic fundamentalism in North Africa and Middle East.

1956 Suez Crisis.

1964 PLO founded with intention to establish Palestinian homeland.

1967 Six-Day War.

1972 Eleven Israeli athletes killed at Munich Olympics.

1973 Yom Kippur War.

1974 PLO limits terrorism to Israel.

1979 Egyptian-Israeli peace deal signed at Camp David.

1994 End of apartheid in South Africa.

1991 End of Cold War.

1990 Gulf War.

c.1990

1989 Communism collapses in Eastern Europe.

1980–1988 Iran-Iraq War.

1987 *Intifada* begins.

1982 Israel invades Lebanon.

c.1980

Glossary

Abbreviations: Arab=Arabic; Heb=Hebrew.

Arabs: A people originating in the Arabian peninsula who now live across northern Africa and southwestern Asia.

bedouin: A nomadic (traveling) people who live in the deserts of north Africa and the Middle East.

Canaan: The ancient land of Israel, covering parts of the present-day state of Israel and the West Bank.

capitalism: An economic system based on supply and demand, and private ownership of businesses and industry.

Christianity: Religion based on the teachings of Jesus Christ.

colonialism: Control of one country or people by another.

communism: A social and political system based on a planned economy in which goods and land are owned by everyone and in which there is no private property.

constitution: A written collection of a country's laws, its citizens' rights, and principal beliefs.

democratic: A process or state where the people choose their government by free elections and where supreme power is held by the people.

export: A product that is sold to another country.

fundamentalism: Religious belief founded on strict adherence to a set of basic principles.

Golan Heights: Area to the northeast of Israel belonging to Syria but currently occupied by Israel.

Hasid: Member of an ultraorthodox group of Jews, originally from Poland.

Hebrews: Ancient people living in what is now modern Israel, the ancestors of the Jewish people.

Hezbollah **(Arab.):** Literally "party of God," guerrilla group in southern Lebanon, opposed to Israeli occupation.

Holocaust: The planned extermination of European Jews by the Nazis during the period 1941–1945.

IDF (abbrev.): Israeli Defence Force, the national army.

Intifada **(Arab.):** Literally "shaking off," the Palestinian rebellion against Israeli rule.

industrial: Describing an economy based on developed industries and infrastructure rather than on agriculture.

Islam: Religion based on the teachings of Mohammed.

Jew: A member or descendant of the Hebrew people;

a person who practices the religion of Judaism.

Judaism: Ancient religion of the Hebrew people.

kibbutz (pl. kibbutzim): Communal agricultural settlement run cooperatively by its members.

Knesset: The Israeli parliament.

kosher: Food prepared according to religious Jewish dietary law.

Koran: The holy book of Islam.

Mohammed: Seventh-century founder of the religion of Islam.

mosque: The religious building of Islam.

Muslim: A follower of Islam.

nationalization: The placing of private industry under government or public control.

oasis: An area of fertile green in the middle of a desert.

Orthodox: Of a religious faith (particularly Judaism), involving strict adherence to religious law.

Ottoman: Turkish empire that ruled Palestine for 400 years.

Palestine: Name that designates eastern Mediterranean area roughly encompassing the modern state of Israel and the West Bank.

PLO (abbrev.): Palestine Liberation Organization.

rabbi: Jewish religious leader and teacher.

Ramadan: Islamic festival commemorating the time when the Koran was revealed to Mohammed.

republic: A government in which the citizens of a country hold political power.

sabrah **(Heb.):** Lit. "prickly pear", native-born Israeli.

shekel: The national currency of Israel.

Sinai: Peninsula in the east of Egypt, largely covered by desert and arid mountains.

socialism: An economic and political system where goods and industry are state owned and where the economy is planned.

synagogue: Jewish religious building and place of learning.

Torah: The first five books of the Hebrew Bible, the most sacred texts of Judaism. Also refers to the "law," the commandments included in these books.

West Bank: Occupied territory west of the Jordan River, originally belonging to Jordan but now ceded by Jordan to the Palestinian people.

Yiddish: Dialect based on medieval German and spoken by Jews living in Eastern Europe.

Bibliography

Major Sources Used for This Book
Bregman, Ahron, El-Tahri, Jihan. *The Fifty Years' War: Israel and the Arabs*. London: BBC Books, 1999.

Gilbert, Martin. *Israel: A History*. New York: William Morrow & Co., 1998.

Sachar, Howard M. *A History of Israel*. New York: Knopf, 1998.\

CIA World Factbook 1998 (www.odci.gov/cia/publications/factbook)

Encyclopedia Britannica

General Further Reading
Encyclopedia of World Cultures ed. Lynda A. Bennett. Boston: G.K. Hall, 1992.

The Kingfisher History Encyclopedia. New York: Kingfisher, 1999.

Student Atlas. New York: Dorling Kindersley, 1998.

The World Book Encyclopedia. Chicago: Scott Fetzer Company, 1999.

World Reference Atlas Dorling Kindersley, London, 2000.

Further Reading About Israel
Fraser, T.G. *The Arab-Israeli Conflict*. New York: St. Martin's Press, 1995.

Gilbert, Martin. *Atlas of Jewish History*. New York: William Morrow & Co., 1993.

Hiro, Dilip. *Sharing the Promised Land*. Interlink Pub. Group, 1999.

Kimmerling, Baruch and Migdak, Joel S. *Palestinians: The Making of a People*. Boston: Harvard University Press, 1994.

Seger, Tom. *1949: The First Israelis*. New York: Henry Holt, 1998.

Some Websites About Israel
www.infotour.co.il (Israeli Government's Tourist Office)

www.israel.org (Israeli Foreign Ministry)

www.visit-palestine.com (Palestinian Ministry of Tourism)

Index

Acknowledgments

Cover Photo Credits
Corbis: Richard T. Nowitz (bedouin woman); Shai
Ginott (Eilat overview); Dave Bartruff (gilt menorah)

Photo Credits
AKG: 67; Erich Lessing 48, 49, 62, 73
Corbis: Archivio Iconografico, S.A. 59; Dave Bartruff
94; Neil Beer 1, 43; Gary Braasch 93 ; Burnstein
Collection 100; Elio Ciol 56; Robert Estall 89; Shai
Ginott 46; Todd Gipstein 65; Historical Picture
Archive 53; Dave G. Houser 69; Hanan Isachar 39,
54; Robbie Jack 97; Steve Kaufman 6, 30, 32; Miki
Kratsman 19; David Lees 61; Charles and Josette

Lenars 23; Buddy Mays 29, 44; Françoise de Mulder
72; Richard T. Nowitz 12, 17, 18, 24, 26, 34, 40, 75,
80, 86, 91, 98, 103, 105, 106, 107, 112; Caroline
Penn 110; David Rubinger 28; Paul A. Souders 36;
Ted Spiegel 85, 99; David H. Wells 74, 102, 116
Hutchison: John Hatt 21; Tony Souter 84
Trip: R. Musallam 38; A. Tovy 16, 22